NUR
FADHILAH WAHID

light upon light

A REFLECTION ON
LIFE, LOVE & GOD

Light upon Light: A Reflection on Life, Love & God

First published in England by
Kube Publishing Ltd, Markfield Conference Centre,
Ratby Lane, Markfield, Leicestershire, LE67 9SY, United Kingdom
Tel: +44 (0) 1530 249230 Fax: +44 (0) 1530 249656
Website: www.kubepublishing.com
Email: info@kubepublishing.com

Cataloguing in-Publication Data is available from the British Library

ISBN Paperback 978-1-84774-123-3
ISBN Ebook 978-1-84774-134-9

Original Cover Design: Nur Fadhilah Binte Wahid
Current Cover Design: Nasir Cadir
Typesetting: Nasir Cadir
Cover Image: iStock
Printed by: MEGA BASIM, Turkey

Dedication

To my mother, who has always believed in me.

To Shaykh Ebrahim Schuitema, whose words and light mended my very broken heart; and to my teachers, who have taught me how to live.

To the too-many-to-count #mashaAllahLadiesinmylife, who have taught me the meaning of love; to the subscribers of 'Letters to Readers', who gave me so much motivation and support to persevere with my writing; and, to my best friend of sixteen years, Atikah Binte Saad, who helped and pushed me to complete the first edition of this book.

Contents

Introduction

Bismillah ir-Rahman ir-Rahim

*Allahumma salli 'ala Sayyidinah Muhammad
wa 'ala alihi wa-sahbihi wa-sallim*

One of the things I love most about sending these letters are the replies I get from readers all around the world—young and old, male and female, Muslims and non-Muslims alike. I could be posting these letters from sunny Singapore or Malaysia, and have someone from Africa, or America, or Europe respond. And for that short moment, we would both be bound together by the same emotions, the emotions I try to capture in my letters; a bond that surpasses whatever differences we might have as individuals. The reader—you—might speak a different language than I, might think in a different way than I, might even have a different understanding of Islam, or perhaps even of God, than I. But in that short moment where my words, my thoughts, and my emotions, resound with yours ... we connect; we share our hopes and fears; we share the struggles we have to be better people; we share the pain of the longing in our hearts.

We begin to see beyond our selves, and we begin to see the human soul that lies within each of us. And for that moment, we love.

***

We live in a time when it is normal to think that everyone is out to take something from us. We go to school thinking we are being educated, when in fact we are being moulded to become unthinking citizens. We work for companies that care nothing about our well-being, but only for their own gains. On a daily basis we fill our minds with content spewed out by media conglomerates who do not care for the quality of our lives, but only for the quantity of their profits. So if we are exposed from a young age to a global culture that, by and large, aims to take as much as possible from us, it is not surprising that we find ourselves clutching onto whatever we perceive is left of our 'selves'.

Allah ...

I remember a conversation I had with Shaykh Ebrahim. He mentioned that the more religion becomes one's identity, the less it is an agent of transformation and change. I was puzzled; shouldn't Islam be one's identity if one is to become a true Muslim?

He smiled, and said (I paraphrase): 'When you think of Islam as an identity, you are, in fact, associating your ideas of what Muslims need to be. When a person has to be a certain way—and no other—then the identity becomes heavy, and thus the religion becomes heavy. Religion is meant to transform us, and to transform, we need to be light.'

The world today is filled with people who cling on to their identities with all their might, thinking that everyone is out to get them. In the Muslim world, all of us form certain ideas of how Islam and Muslims should be. Because we form our identities around these ideas—and after all our identities are the only possession we have left that is within 'our control'—we find ourselves rejecting all other thoughts different from ours, even if they are derived from the Qur'an, Sunnah, ijma' of the 'ulama', and through qiyas.

Four years ago, when I first returned to Islam, I dressed myself in a certain 'Islamic' way and became almost tyrannical in protecting my notion of what Islam is, and in the process, became extremely judgmental of others ... whether I realized it or not. In the words of my best friend: 'You were so overbearing with your religiosity and your beliefs; it was hard for me to be with you.' And it showed—even if I was too blind to see it then—for my first two years on campus, I barely made any new friends; I was too 'heavy' to be around.

A few weeks ago I attended a class on *fiqh* meant for the general public. During the class, the ustadh began to criticize other groups that had a different understanding of the religion, and he started to openly mock the actions of some people in the class ... all the while sharing the 'rightfulness' of his Islam. By the end of the class, I found out that many had withdrawn from it—even those who were 'new' to the religion and really wanted to learn. The truth is that the world today is filled with broken hearts (including mine), and whether we realize it or not, our hearts long for the nourishment of the Light and the moment of unity with the True Love.

When we, as a people, hold on to our identities and force them upon others, we are breaking more hearts as we subconsciously look down on them. We are hurting them too, as we force them into 'square holes' despite the various shapes and sizes they come in. In this way we dilute Islam into an identity—our identity—instead of allowing it to be the powerful tool of change and transformation that it is.

The alternative to this is to look beyond our selves—or our so-called identities—and to start looking into souls. We need to see not just the shape and manifestation of things, but to see the underlying meanings of each. In this world, where everyone is out to take from the other, we need to surrender our own agenda, and to learn to truly give. And in moments we manage to do this, broken hearts get mended … and broken hearts begin to love.

***

Struck a chord?

Any time you feel like you resound with the letters and have something to share with me and other readers, don't hesitate to get in touch using the hashtag #lightuponlightbyfw.

1

A Quarter of a Century

Bismillah ir-Rahman ir-Rahim

Today, I turn twenty-five.

Yesterday, by the grace of Allah, I stumbled across several of my diaries dating back to 2004. As I was flipping from one page to another, I came across several du'a's I made. In one of the du'a's—a silly one—I prayed that He would grant me the enjoyment of the Dunya before bringing me back close to Him. I was young and naive, and I wanted to taste the pleasures of the world. I made a whole list of items that I perceived would bring me happiness, and as I read the list today, I realized that over the years He had granted me all, save for one, of what I had asked for; both the good things, and the bad. After ticking off the entire checklist here I am today, knocking on His door.

In another du'a', I asked that He open my heart to wear the hijab once again upon my entrance into university. In defiance, at age fifteen I had taken off the hijab I had worn since I was a child and gave myself until I was eighteen to sort out my life. But at eighteen, I had flunked my A-levels and did not earn a place at the local university. I started working full time, without any intention to pursue my studies, and wearing the hijab was the last thing on my mind. Little did I know, seven years after making the du'a', He placed me in a university, and with it placed the hijab again in my heart.

The reason I am sharing this with you is that it struck me that Allah subhanahu wa ta'ala truly listens to every single one of our du'a's. No matter if the du'a' is one made in passing or one that is made consistently, He is always listening. What this means is that we should be more careful of the words that slip off our tongue; those that are directed to ourselves, as well as those directed to others. What this also means, more importantly, is that we have to realize that our du'a's for ourselves today will shape who we are tomorrow. Our du'a's will shape the kind of person we will become, the relationships we will have, and the lives we will one day lead. What then, will our du'a's be? What then, will your du'a's be?

May He gift us the ability to make du'a's that are good for us in the Dunya and Akhirah, amin!

2

Becoming Gordon Ramsay

Bismillah ir-Rahman ir-Rahim

Sometime last semester, my friends and I came across a video of Gordon Ramsay's *Kitchen Nightmares* and we voted to watch it while eating our lunch. We loved the episode so much—clearly made for cheap entertainment—that we decided to watch all of the episodes (and seasons) during our lunch breaks and dinners in the days to come.

So every single day—twice a day—as we dug into our food, we watched as Gordon Ramsay turned restaurants upside down. He would come in, scrutinize each of the dishes served, and make blistering comments peppered generously with vulgarities. Our dates with him went on undisturbed for weeks, until one evening we decided to eat out at a restaurant off-campus.

The Night of Transformation

The restaurant was empty when we entered it, save for a small family of three seated in the middle of the room. We were quickly ushered to a corner booth, where the waiters took our orders without much fanfare and made for the kitchen.

'Where are all the other customers?' One of us asked.
'I don't know. Maybe it says something about the food here?'
'Then why are we eating here?' We laughed and the conversation turned to other topics.

Barely minutes later, we heard a 'ding!' coming from the kitchen, and a waiter walked out with our first dish: spaghetti carbonara. He placed it deftly on our table, slid the cutlery over, and returned to the kitchen as another 'ding!' echoed around the empty restaurant.

My forehead scrunched as I looked at the plate before me. Comment after pithy comment blazed through my mind: 'Soggy. Too thick. Flooded with too much sauce. Bad presentation.' I touched the plate. It was cold. 'Must be microwaved.' My fingers reached for the fork and I found myself jabbing the food, trying to find the spaghetti immersed under all the sauce. I was becoming increasingly annoyed and agitated, and when the spaghetti finally entered my mouth, my lips gave way to a frown. I let out a sigh, meeting the gaze of my roommates: 'Not worth it.'

The waiter came to our table again. I resisted the urge to complain about the food and concentrated on swishing my spaghetti around on the plate. He placed the next dish on the table: a calamari plate. As soon as he was gone, I watched my friend as her face, like mine, broke into a frown. She picked up the fork and began separating the array of fried seafood on the plate. There were only three pieces of calamari. I saw her struggle to keep her comments to herself. She picked up one of the calamari, fed it into her mouth, and began chewing. Seconds later, the food came out again. Meeting my gaze, she explained with a tinge of irritation, 'too much flour. Tastes weird.'

When the third dish arrived—seconds after another 'ding!' from the kitchen—we looked at the plate before us and scrunched our foreheads. We grabbed a spoonful, tasted it, and begun making comments again, completely dissatisfied. Only then did it strike me that we were acting exactly like Gordon Ramsay in *Kitchen Nightmares*.

Cultivation Theory

In media studies, there exists an idea called the 'cultivation theory'. To put it simply, this explains how when someone watches television over time, the content they watch affects their own thoughts and actions; they are more likely to believe social reality aligns with the 'reality' portrayed on television. One of the most quoted research in the area is that of television violence and its effect on children. Results after results of duplicated research have shown that children's tendency to act violently is directly related to watching violence on television; the more they watch violent programmes, the more they are likely to act violently. Similarly, after weeks of watching Gordon Ramsay's behaviour towards food, my friends and I were wiring ourselves to emulate the very same behaviour when faced with food in a restaurant. Without realizing it, from the moment we entered the empty restaurant, to the times we heard the distinct 'ding!' from the kitchen (a sign of bad food in any *Kitchen Nightmares* episode), to the point where we jabbed the food and tasted it critically, we were all merely re-enacting what we saw.

Just as what we eat becomes a part of our body, what we consume through our eyes and ears become a part of us, affecting our thoughts and behaviour. *'Tell the believing men to lower their gaze and guard their modesty; that is more purifying for them. Surely Allah is aware of what they do'*. (al-Nur 24: 30) So the next time you turn on the television, or spend time watching videos on YouTube, ask yourself: 'Do I want to be like those I'm watching?'

3

The Best Reminder of Life

Bismillah ir-Rahman ir-Rahim

I was at the cemetery yesterday, watching and making du'a' as the excavator gently lowered soil into the grave holding my aunt. I watched as the soil tumbled into the hole, covering the wooden plank inch by inch, until finally my relatives poured water over the grave and made their final du'a's. I watched as my cousins cried at the passing of their mother, as their children teared up at the death of their grandmother, and as my mother struggled to hold back her own tears as she said goodbye to her sister for the last time. And in the middle of all of that, I watched as my whole life ran through my mind—the decisions I have made, the dreams and aspirations I hold on to and, most importantly, the relationships I have made and broken.

Many of us, deep down in our hearts, know what the important things in life are. We know that above everything else is our relationship with Allah subhanahu wa ta'ala and the Prophet Muhammad *sallallahu 'alayhi wa sallam,* and our relationship with the people around us— our parents, our siblings, our relatives, our friends and the whole of mankind. And yet, in living life we tend to let urgent matters get in the way of the things we know are important.

Without realizing it, we turn our backs on those who love us, in order to chase after deadlines. We keep ourselves busy with our careers and our bosses, and spend little time with our family and friends. We invest so much energy in achieving 'success', as it is understood generally, but give only remnants of what is left to the 'success' that Allah subhanahu wa ta'ala refers to—the one in this world and the Hereafter. And yet, it is Allah subhanahu wa ta'ala who grants us life, and it is the people we leave behind that will make du'a' for us even after our 'life' is taken away from us. The companion of the Prophet Muhammad *sallallahu 'alayhi wa sallam,* 'Umar al-Khattab *radhiallahu 'anhu,* used to wear a ring engraved with the phrase: 'Death is enough an admonisher.' As I walked back to the car and to my life, the phrase kept on ringing in my head, forcing me to re-evaluate my decisions and my actions over the past few months.

If I were to die today, how would I describe my relationship with Allah subhanahu wa ta'ala? How would I describe my relationship with my family, my friends, and others? *Alhamdulillah,* painful as it is to ask myself these questions, it was like I was given a chance to live again. Make that reflection. Take that small step. Send that message to your old friend. Rekindle that relationship with the sibling you fell out with. Tell someone how much you appreciate them being in your life. Perhaps one day, *insha' Allah*, they will be watching and making du'a' for you when the soil tumbles into your last abode ...

May Allah subhanahu wa ta'ala keep us in His Love and Mercy, in His guidance and protection, and may He place my aunt, Hajah Sa'yah Bte Haji Soib, among His beloved. Amin!

4

How to be Happy with your Self

Bismillah ir-Rahman ir-Rahim

Two years ago, I remember envying my roommate to the extent that I hated speaking or even looking at her. This was an extremely big deal, as we were close friends and I had entered university only because she had agreed to join me. I envied Sajaf, as I will call her,[1] because she was always so soft-spoken and gentle, always the first to help others, and doing good deeds came naturally to her. I, on the other hand, was rough and stern, and I struggled immensely when it came to doing *'ibadah* (worship) and placing the needs of others above mine.

One morning, I decided to wake up earlier than all my other roommates so that I could surprise them with breakfast. I knew

---

1. Throughout this book, names and identifying details have been changed to protect the privacy of individuals.

everyone's morning routine by heart, and I had timed my alarm accordingly. However, when I woke up and stepped out of my room, I saw Sajaf crouching over our small pantry. She glanced at me, smiled, and said: 'Good morning! I decided to make breakfast for all of you!' I walked out of the room. Disappointed. Angry. Envious. Hateful, even. 'Such a show off,' I muttered under my breath, 'Why must she act like she is better than everyone else?' I failed to realize that the only person who was acting (up) in that situation was me; Sajaf was only being herself.

To some of you reading this, what I went through may sound extreme, and in many ways, it was. But when I shared this thought with my confidantes, we quickly realized that to various degrees many of us go through the same process. When we see someone scoring As when we get Bs, we feel a pang in our heart. When we see someone climbing the corporate ladder like it was on fire, our guts burn from the jealousy we feel. When we see someone travelling the world as if money was no object, writing awesome things and taking fantastic photos, we feel like the world has short-changed us.

Some of us react by projecting hatred and anger towards ourselves, by feeling upset and depressed, thinking how useless we are. Others may react like I did, and start projecting hatred and anger towards the other person, leading to gossip and ill-thought. From this, a smaller minority actualize their hatred by resorting to damaging actions like *sihr* (black magic) or sabotage. Whatever the outcome of the feelings of envy we feel, in actuality the root of envy is discontentment with ourselves, and the feeling that we can only be complete if we have … (insert whatever ideal).

What if, today, we throw away this discontentment we have with ourselves? What if instead of looking at the awesomeness of others, we find our own awesomeness that Allah subhanahu wa ta'ala has placed within us? What if instead of beating ourselves up for not being a certain way, we celebrate the goodness within us and amplify that goodness instead? The Prophet Muhammad *sallallahu 'alayhi wa sallam* used to give different advice to different companions because he understood how everyone was unique and had their own struggles and strengths. For example, Sayyidina 'Umar *radhiallahu 'anhu* was known to be stern, just as Sayyidina 'Uthman *radhiallahu 'anhu* was known to be gentle. We often forget that 'Umar did not have to be like 'Uthman in order to get the love of the Prophet Muhammad *sallallahu 'alayhi wa sallam*, and neither did 'Uthman have to be like 'Umar. They both just worked towards being the best person they could be.

Two days ago, my friends and I had a gathering at Sajaf's place. As I stepped into her home, I found her crouched over her kitchen pantry, smiling at me: 'Good morning! I prepared appetisers, lunch and dessert for all of you!' I walked into the kitchen, happily stuffed a freshly-baked pastry into my mouth, and then helped her fill the ice box. And then I came home and wrote this letter to you ... because writing is what I am good at.

May Allah subhanahu wa ta'ala grant us the understanding of ourselves, the ability to be thankful for all He has given us, and the patience and guidance to strive to be the best version of ourselves. Amin!

5

Who Do We Turn To?

Bismillah ir-Rahman ir-Rahim

The rain water swirled around my feet before entering my shoes and drenching me to the bone. My flimsy umbrella was no match for the heavy downpour; I was wet from head to toe and so was my spirit. I glanced worriedly at the watch strapped on my wrist, its clear surface pockmarked with drops of rain, distorting the numbers beneath. It had been thirty minutes since I first stood by the road, waiting for a cab, and I was left with forty-five minutes or so to get to the bus station, a journey I knew would be punctuated by a series of traffic jams. I began to worry.

I reached for my mobile phone, punching in numbers to call for a cab. I sighed in frustration as cabs filled with passengers went past me, seemingly mocking my situation, and the automated voice at the end of the line kept telling me to wait for what seemed like a lifetime. I heaved a sigh of annoyance and trudged further down the road, anxious and heavy-hearted. When I finally got to the end of the road, the automated voice told me that no cabs were available and that I should 'try again later'.

Feeling like all of this was beyond anything I could manage, I closed my eyes and made a prayer: 'O my Lord, make things easier for me, do not make things difficult for me. O My Lord, let my affairs end with goodness.' I opened my eyes and I kid you not, a cab made a last-minute turn at the junction and rolled up in front of me. When I finally settled on the back seat, the driver turned around and quipped: 'Why didn't you flag down the cab? I couldn't really see you in the downpour and was about to make a right turn, but something told me to turn left. I could have missed you!' *Subhan Allah.*

The incident reminded me of the advice I once received from a friend. She said that we, in facing any problems in life, tend to occupy ourselves with excessive worry, seeking solutions or assistance from others. In doing so, we fool ourselves by thinking that we, or others, can solve our problems for us. The reality is that it was Allah subhanahu wa ta'ala who put us into that situation, and it is only He who can remove that situation for us.

So why do we waste time and energy seeking help from those other than the One from whom all things originate? For the rest of the week, let us try to make Allah subhanahu wa ta'ala the first thought we have when we face any kind of problems—from our dealings with people, with finances, with situations and mostly, with ourselves. Let us try our best to complain of our shortcomings and woes to Him first, before anyone or anything else. May Allah subhanahu wa ta'ala let us see the wisdom behind seemingly 'bad' incidents happening to us, and may He make it easy for us to go through trying times. Amin!

6

Lesson from a Homeless Man

Bismillah ir-Rahman ir-Rahim

The old man's left arm twitched as he struggled to align the pieces of canvas in front of him. My friends and I paused to read what he was about to write, and on noticing our presence, the old man began to speak. It was hard trying to understand what he was saying; there was a live band playing just metres away and he was mumbling his words, stringing them together into one long sentence without beginning or end. I sat on the steps next to him, leaning in, trying to make out the words. I could make out the word 'shi'ah', a minister's name, and after five minutes I had all but passed off his words as those spoken by a rambling madman. Besides, the live band had started playing a song I used to love listening to.

Then the old man began to write, his right hand determined to stay on course as his left jerked. It seemed to me as if he had to use his entire strength and soul to put ink on canvas; his legs were bent in an awkward manner and his whole body shook and swayed in tandem with the strokes of his black marker: 'Bismillah'—in the name of Allah. But why on earth was he writing with the letters facing away from him?

'It's not that I cannot write as people usually do. I can, and it's much easier to do that. But when I write with the letters facing you instead of facing me, doesn't it make it easier for you to read and understand it? I should make things easier for you to understand, even if it makes it harder for me ...'. I was taken aback by his answer to the question in my head. I began to chide myself for having such ill thoughts of him just seconds earlier. The music from the band seemed to become louder, but as I threw my attention towards the old man and commanded my heart to listen, his words seemed to make more sense. I began to realize it was just me who did not want to listen to him in the first place.

'I don't live here. In fact, I am from pretty far away. But I walked all the way from where I was to where I am, making *dhikr* (remembrance of Allah subhanahu wa ta'ala) all the way, asking only for one thing: that Allah subhanahu wa ta'ala will let me see the beauty of the moon tonight. Even so, I have yet to see the moon. But it's ok, because we don't always get what we want in life. We just have to continue making remembrance of Allah subhanahu wa ta'ala and we will be ok.'

Fifteen minutes later, my friends and I made our move and got him to make du'a' for us. We retreated back onto the main street, silent and reflecting on what the old man had just taught us. First, in life, it might be much easier to do things the way we want to, but it is much more beneficial to do things the way they need to be done. For example, it is easy to advise someone by nagging at them or making an off-the-cuff comment, but it takes much more effort and patience to advise them with wisdom, at the right moment, gently, in the best way possible. Second, even though we can strive to do all we can and make all the du'a' in the world, we have to learn to be content with what Allah subhanahu wa ta'ala has given us and trust that He will give us what is best for us. We have to learn to say, live, and breathe *Alhamdulillah*. Lastly, no matter how poor or rich you are, no matter how low or high your social status is, no matter whether you're homeless or live in a palace, honour can only be given to those Allah subhanahu wa ta'ala wills it for. So much speaks of the heart that dismissed a man's speech just because of his outer appearance, and so much speaks of the heart that gives thanks to Allah subhanahu wa ta'ala even in the most dire of situations.

As my friends and I continued down the street, I looked up into the night sky and saw the full moon in its glory. Perhaps the old man will get his du'a' granted after all.

May we be that person who relies only on Allah subhanahu wa ta'ala and strives only for His *rida*, amin!

7

Picking Yourself Up and Moving Forward

Bismillah ir-Rahman ir-Rahim

'As-salamu Aalaykum, Shaykh Yahya.' My friend's voice filled the hall: 'We have been liberal all our lives and it is only two to three years ago that we tried to become better Muslims. We try so hard, but some days we find our past haunts us so much that we begin to lose hope in everything and fall back to our old ways. It's so hard, Shaykh, to pick ourselves up when we start walking down our past. Could you share with us how we can keep on moving forward instead of taking three steps forward and two steps back?'

Shaykh Yahya smiled upon hearing our question, or rather, our complaint of our selves: 'Allah, Allah. Just pick yourself up, wipe the dust off, and move forward. Satan will always place doubt in your hearts, telling you to lose hope and go back to your old ways, especially when you are down. Just ignore him, pick yourself up and keep moving forward. (Shows action of wiping dust off hands) Don't dwell. Pick yourself up, and keep moving forward.' It struck me that I already knew the answer to my own question, I had written about it, after all, but somehow I still needed someone else to tell me what to do. Why? Why do I do that? Why do we do that?

Why do we need someone to answer all of our questions, even though we already know the answers deep within our heart? We know that we just have to tell ourselves 'no', and move forward. But we keep on avoiding it, because when we are at rock-bottom we are blinded by the darkness and the climb back up just feels so tiresome and cumbersome. We ask because we want someone to give us a short cut, a magic du'a' or advice that will magically bring us and our *iman* back up to its soaring height.

But, guess what? Life is all about that gruelling climb; there are no short cuts! And once we accept this, once we learn to not resist the climb, only then will we find sweetness and joy in the act of climbing. With each fall, we learn something new about ourselves and we can take steps not to go down the same route again. And we have to keep on doing this—falling, dusting ourselves off, and keep on climbing—until we realize that over time, it gets easier to pick ourselves up and we actually begin to appreciate the falls and the lessons we learn from them.

There is no short cut, no magic du'a', no miracle advice. It is the same in matters of our *iman*, just as it is the same in other things in life, like remoulding our character, or even getting work done. We just have to dust ourselves off and keep moving forward. Choose not to dwell. Choose to make your way back up. Choose to remember that Allah's mercy prevails over His wrath. Imam Ibn Athaillah Rahimahullah said: 'One of the signs of delusion is sadness over the loss of obedience, coupled with an absence of resolve to bring it back to life.'

May He make it easy for us to be reminded of His Mercy and Love, *insha' Allah*!

8

A Side of Me You Didn't Know

Bismillah ir-Rahman ir-Rahim

The truth about me is that I am constantly living in self-doubt and fear. When I graduated as the top Malay student in my primary school, with a PSLE score high enough to get me into the best school in Singapore, I chose to go to a neighbourhood (albeit autonomous) school. When I went through secondary school, surrounded by classmates who were the crème de la crème in that school, I chose instead to hang out with some bad company, who did not make studies a priority. When I went to college, I spent most of my days skipping classes, changing out of my uniform and heading to the nearest dodgy basement-shop; with pool tables and weird smells wafting from the couches lining the walls. In making all of those decisions, I realize now that it was because I wanted to remain in a safe place. In my mind, I told myself over and over again that my PSLE score meant that I was intelligent, and it is only out of my own personal choice that I was living an average life. I could have been a doctor, a lawyer, a professor, but I chose to be average because I prefer the simple life.

I'm calling your bluff, Fadhilah. I made those decisions because I was afraid that being in an environment where everyone was 'the same' as me would eventually mean that I would no longer be the best. I wanted to be the best, but the only way I thought I could remain being the best was to be somewhere there was no competition. By default, I would be the winner, since I would be the only one in that category. When I no longer had a choice to be in a different environment, I chose not to compete. I sat by the tracks and watched everyone run by, thinking, 'I could win if I wanted to, but I would prefer not to.'

A few months back, a sister sent me an email asking for my opinion on where she should pursue her degree. I told her that it would be better if she went to University X instead of University Y, because University X had a better programme, a better faculty, and a better reputation, generally. A few days later she replied that she had chosen to go to University Y, because if University Y was so bad it would be easier for her to sail through the programme and be the best student there.

I was upset with her way of thinking. How could she improve and be better if she chose to remain where she was? Why did she want to fool herself into thinking she's the best when in reality it is only the circumstance that gives her the illusion of being the best? Why didn't she think that perhaps, if she enrolled into University X and worked hard, she could still be the best student, *bismillah*? Then it would mean that she truly is the best! Then it dawned on me that perhaps that email was delivered by Allah subhanahu wa ta'ala straight to my heart, to get me thinking about my own life. *Allahu akbar*, He sure works in mysterious ways.

Why am I sharing this with you? Because I know there are many others who are like me, people who can be brilliant in their own way, but choose to remain average out of the fear of failing, the fear of success, the fear of the unknown, or even the fear of discovering who they really are. What if it turns out that I am not really intelligent after all? What if I actually can't cook although I want to be a chef? What if the only reason my relatives bought my artwork is because they love me? What if I step out of my bubble and the world out there hurts too much? The truth is that no one gets to become the first in the race by sitting next to the tracks. The truth is that we need to learn to walk, and then fall, and then pick ourselves up again, and keep on running and falling, until one day we actually enjoy the run itself. It does not matter if we come in first, second, or way behind, because the fact that we are running is already a win compared to just watching the world go by.

This semester I finally forced myself to do a couple of things I've wanted to do for a long time but resisted out of fear. Some days I laugh, because I know I am just making things up as I go along, and most days I have to use all of my will power to just tell myself to stop fearing and doubting myself. It's tough, it's painful, and I am still crawling at best. But I am finally moving, and the air is fresher than when I was still.

May Allah subhanahu wa ta'ala give us the strength to break away from our self-induced slumber and to grow, amin!

9

who Do You Want to Be?

Bismillah ir-Rahman ir-Rahim

I was watching an episode of *Suits* this afternoon when one of the things Harvey Specter said lodged itself in my mind. Harvey Specter is the protagonist of the show; a highly-skilled lawyer with a reputation that would send shivers down the spine of any other lawyer in town. In this episode, he was commanded by his superior to do something that was against his beliefs. He flat out refused, even though it would mean he would lose his position, and when asked by another why he would risk all that, he said: 'It's not about what I want to do. It's also not about where I want to be. In the end, it's about who I want to be.'

Who Do You Want To Be?

In a book I read recently about habits, the author said that it is much easier for people to start changing themselves and their habits by first thinking about the person they want to be. The change of habits will naturally follow suit later. So instead of diving in to pray *tahajjud* every night, first seed the intention that, 'I want to be a better Muslimah'. Instead of downloading ten apps for running (guilty as charged), first seed the intention that 'I want to be a healthy person'. Instead of allocating an hour of play-time with your children, first seed the intention that 'I want to be the best parent ever!'

The beauty of first having the intention and vision of who you want to be is that your change is not limited to the actions you have planned in mind. Instead, your change is guided by your intention and vision, and that is a much more powerful driving force than checking off to-do lists. When you intend and envision yourself to be in a certain way, when you truly believe with your whole heart and see with your eyes the person you want to be, then all the actions you take or refuse to take, will be in harmony. It will motivate you to pray *tahajjud* every night, it will question you—'Really, Fadhilah? Really?'—when you reach for that third doughnut in one sitting, it will cheer you on when you spend time with your children, even when you are exhausted after a whole day of work. So think about it: Who do you want to be? Get the answer, then start being the answer.

May Allah subhanahu wa ta'ala reveal to us the person we are meant to be, and may He gift us the strength to be shaped into that person by His loving, moulding Hands, amin!

10

The True Story of Maarop Mohd Noh

Bismillah ir-Rahman ir-Rahim

One of my lecturers loves to tell stories in class, from his adventures being a journalist to his time being the Prime Minister's right hand man. But out of all his stories, the ones that he loves to tell the most are about a man named Maarop Mohd Noh. With his permission, on this blessed morning I would like to share one of those stories with you, *insha' Allah*.

***

I remember once when I was with him (Maarop Mohd Noh) walking along a stretch of road. We were walking while having a conversation, when he stopped in his tracks and looked down at his flip-flops. He bent over and retrieved a small stone that had gone into his flip-flops and was hurting his foot. Instead of just tossing it aside, he did something I have never seen anyone do: he kissed it, before setting it back at the side of the road. Then he put his flip-flops on, and continued walking.

I caught up next to him in silence, but my curiosity drove me to ask: 'Why did you kiss that stone?'

Maarop Mohd Noh turned to me, smiled, and said: 'I am thanking the stone for giving me a reminder from Allah subhanahu wa ta'ala for all the mistakes I have made.'

Whenever a Muslim is afflicted with a hardship, sickness, sadness, worry, harm, or depression—even a thorn's prick—Allah expiates his sins because of it. (Hadith Bukhari)

May we begin our week with the intention to be thankful to Allah subhanahu wa ta'ala for everything good and bad that happens to us, *insha' Allah*. Amin!

11

Want an Easy Life?
Don't Get Close to Allah!

(Yes, I am serious.)

Bismillah ir-Rahman ir-Rahim

An old friend came to me, distraught. She is the type of person who always gets everything she wants, and if she does not get it by 'pure luck', then she would do everything within her means to get it: A close-knit family, a managing role in an international firm, a fully-fledged business, and a lifestyle that many would envy—you could say that she has it all. She would even say to me: 'I'm lucky. I have always gotten anything that I desire.'

In the past few months, my friend had taken it upon herself to rediscover Islam. She relearnt how to pray, started going to the mosque, and even began fasting every Monday and Thursday. There was something that Islam brought to her life that she could not get in any of her other activities; life was wonderful for a while, and she kept making one *sujud shukr* (a prostration out of gratitude) after another. But recently things began to fall apart. She would get a big business deal, make *sujud shukr*, and find out that the next day the deal had fallen through. Then she would find out about someone slandering her behind her back. And just as suddenly as she received a huge sum of money, some bills would come from nowhere and all the money just evaporated into thin air. 'It's like, the more I try to become a true Muslim, the more I try to get closer to Allah subhanahu wa ta'ala, the harder life gets!'

Looking back at my own journey, I can see how true her statement is. I used to not give a hoot about anyone around me, going about doing all the things I wanted to without a care in the world. I would not give a thought about the words I said or the actions I took or the loved ones I hurt. I had money in the bank; I went for holidays, shopped till I dropped, and I had with me the company of a person I thought was the love of my life. I was blissfully happy and carefree. I was set for life.

However, when I returned to Islam, I lost my relationship, gave up my job, and moved to a new country to seek knowledge, away from the comforts of my normal life. I began to notice the negative character traits I had, and every single day I battled with myself to turn over a new leaf. For months I didn't have many new friends, and I would call my best friend, crying, wanting to return home. I was angry with Allah subhanahu wa ta'ala, and I was confused. Isn't the world supposed to be a better place when you walk towards Him?

Actually, no. The path of hardship and trial is the path of the Prophets and the *salihin* (the righteous ones). Prophet Muhammad *sallallahu 'alayhi wa sallam*, despite his closeness to Allah subhanahu wa ta'ala, was placed in poverty, mocked by those close to him, and even found himself being pelted with stones by young children. The fact is that the more hardship and trials you go through in this world, the more you find yourself less enchanted by what the world has to offer. And the more disenchanted you get with the world, the more you turn towards Allah, towards that which is everlasting.

I realize today that when you start walking towards Allah subhanahu wa ta'ala, He runs towards you. And in the process, the world falls far behind until all that is left is only Allah and you. And after all the struggles and the hardship, when you have finally rid yourself of the love of the life of this world, only then will you find true ease with Allah subhanahu wa ta'ala. Until then, welcome to the path of hardship, the path of the Prophets and the *salihin*.

May Allah subhanahu wa ta'ala gift us with the eyes to see the wisdom behind the tribulations He places on our path, the patience and strength to go through them, and the gratitude that comes with overcoming them, amin!

12

What is better than Your Today?

Bismillah ir-Rahman ir-Rahim

I love new beginnings. I love the crisp crunch of a new notebook, and flipping through all the blank pages just waiting to be filled in. I love the excitement of a new semester, looking through the list of modules and knowing I will get a fresh start to be a better student. I love the mystery of a new year, a break from all that has passed and a chance to start anew.

At the time of writing, today ushers in the year 1435 AH in the Islamic calendar. The Hijrah calendar serves as a reminder of the Prophet's migration from Makkah to Madinah, a reminder for us to make the hijrah (migration) of our spiritual selves. In lieu of the new year, I propose a challenge to all of us: Let us choose one Sunnah of the Prophet *sallallahu 'alayhi wa sallam*—the smallest, simplest Sunnah that is easiest for you—and start doing it today.

It can be something you have long forgotten, like making the du'a' before sleeping, or it can be something you have wanted to do for a long while, like waking up for *tahajjud* (the night prayer) or giving money to charity every day. Start doing it daily, and start logging your progress. Once you are comfortable with your new habit, add another Sunnah you want to inculcate.

Shaykh Hamza Yusuf recommended doing an action for forty consecutive days for it to become embedded in you, whilst a recent Western text mentions five consecutive days. Choose whichever you are comfortable with. Research has shown that as you slowly succeed in developing new habits, your ability to take on more new habits is strengthened exponentially. And when this happens, as we keep on improving day by day in the smallest way possible, we are answering the question in the title of this letter: What is better than your today? The answer: Your tomorrow, *insha' Allah*.

> **'Your today must be better than yesterday,**
> **or else you have deteriorated'.**
> —Prophet Muhammad *sallallahu 'alayhi wa sallam*

May Allah subhanahu wa ta'ala forgive the sins we have committed knowingly or unknowingly in the past year, and may He make it easy for us to follow the footsteps of our beloved Prophet *sallallahu 'alayhi wa sallam*. Amin!

13

The Reason Why I Couldn't Write at All

Bismillah ir-Rahman ir-Rahim

This past week, I haven't been writing at all. I would sit at my desk, open my laptop, and rest my fingers on the keyboard. A word or two would stutter out, but just as suddenly as they came, I would reach out to the 'delete' button and erase what I had written. The screen remained clean and white and empty and I would just sit in silence, my usually noisy brain letting out barely a hum.

But my heart thumped. Boy, did my heart thump! You see, in a beautifully (*wallah*, beautiful) planned series of events by Allah subhanahu wa ta'ala, last week a book by Shaykh Ebrahim Etsko Schuitema titled *The Millennium Discourses* landed in my hands. *Insha' Allah*, I will share the brilliant story with you one day, but for now, because I really am rendered speechless as I keep revisiting Shaykh

Ebrahim's words, I'd just like to share an excerpt (out of countless excerpts) that I fell in love with:

> He is the author and the only reason He has written all of this, is so that we can appreciate the story. The whole universe that you are presented with is a story that is written for you for one reason only, for your appreciation and delight. This is why He has written it. He has done it all to enchant you.

> His creation is therefore the supreme act of love, the supreme manifestation of generosity. He informs us that He has done all of this because He wants to share His wonders. Because, who is He? He is the Hidden Treasure which proclaims 'I love to be known'. He is the Wonderful, He is the Majestic, and that is what He wants to share with you.

> He grants you your existence from Him so that He can share His with you, so that you may be delighted.[2]

Subhan Allah, walhamdulillah!

Some of you have asked me for book recommendations, and honest to goodness, out of all the books I have read this past year, I would say get this one. It has changed so much of the way I was thinking and feeling about myself and the world, and *Alhamdulillah*, several other friends who bought the book said the same as well. In fact, my

---

2. Etsko Schuitema, *The Millennium Discourses* (Edinburgh: Intent Publishing, 2011).

best friend made an overseas call to me just to share how much the book had affected her (in a good way)!

For those of you who want to improve your relationship with Allah subhanahu wa ta'ala and the people around you, who would like to truly understand why we go through trials and tribulations, who would like know the reason you are here in this world, read the book.

***

Author's note: What happened was that I was at a stage in my life where I was really down and needed a lot of motivation to get back up. Thus I devoured one Western self-help book after another, and in many ways they lifted my spirits. However, one evening as I passed by Wardah Books (a quaint, most amazing, Sufi bookstore in Arab Street, Singapore), my heart tugged at me to enter and ask for 'Islamic self-help', whatever that was. *Alhamdulillah*, Sidi Ibrahim, the bookstore owner, was in, and as he listened to me gushing about the self-help books I had been reading, he traced his fingers along the spines of his books until he came to the book that changed much of my life: *Millennium Discourses*, by Shaykh Etsko Schuitema. Handing the book over, he casually said, 'Perhaps you should not read those self-help books you talk about. One day you'll understand why.'

Today, as I reflect back on his words, I understand the dangers of self-help books: the emphasis on the 'self'. Such books often call to one's ego—'I' can do this, 'I' can do that, 'I' am the one in charge. But, isn't God in charge? Isn't God the enabler of all things? Isn't God the arranger of all affairs? Therein lies the subtle deceit of self-help books, for the ones that do not notice it. In order to live a contented life, we need to stop thinking that we are in charge, and rather submit to God and let Him take charge! Self-help vs God's help!

Case-in-point: While I was searching for self-help books, I was also searching for a place to intern at, as my university life was coming to an end. *Alhamdulillah*, I did well in school and was offered several opportunities in various media companies within Malaysia. But my heart was not happy in taking them up, because that would mean writing for things that may or may not fall into the folds of what I believe in. I became frustrated in my search for alternatives and was about to give up and give in, when my mother reminded me: 'Just pray for what you want, Fadhilah. *Insha' Allah*, He will provide.' And so I gave up my search even with the deadline looming.

Fast-forwarding the story, after I read Shaykh Ebrahim's book and gushed about it all over my letters and Facebook status updates, an email came in from ... guess who? A Singaporean who was working with Shaykh Ebrahim in South Africa! And ... after a few emails and messages back and forth, Shaykh Ebrahim offered me an all-expenses paid internship in his company in South Africa, writing about all the things I believed in. God helps! *Alhamdulillah*.

14

The Secret to Being Content All the Time

Bismillah ir-Rahman ir-Rahim

I have a friend who says '*Alhamdulillah*' all the time. When she plans for something and it doesn't work out, she says *Alhamdulillah*. When the doctor told her that her husband had a form of permanent illness, she said *Alhamdulillah*. A couple of weeks later, she discovered that she had a growth in her body. Guess what she said? '*Alhamdulillah*,' she smiled. I couldn't understand it. There I was, feeling all, 'woe is me, woe is me!' every time I had something as minor as the flu. And there she was, smiling and saying *Alhamdulillah* to every single thing. 'What's the secret?' I asked. I wanted the elixir of happiness, I wanted the power to be above the storms of life and to emerge unperturbed. I wanted the secret to being content all the time.

'It is not about what you want for yourself. It is about accepting and being grateful of what Allah wants for you,' she advised.

It was like she could read my thoughts. And it was like they were being thrown back in my face. Ouch.

Today, I walked to campus in the afternoon. The sun was right overhead, and I was sweating buckets. My left shoe had a hole in it, and random gravel would get in and poke into my foot, making walking uncomfortable. I did not feel like going to class as I was nursing a stomach ache. But my lecturer had emphasized that there would be class today, so I went all the same. I put on my headphones and began the fifteen-minute walk accompanied by Shaykh Hamza Yusuf. At one point, he said:

> The Prophet *sallallahu ʻalayhi wa sallam* once saw a woman nursing her child. And he said to a companion, 'Do you think this woman would throw her child into the fire?' And the companion said, 'Wallahi, Rasulullah, she would never do that!' And he *sallallahu ʻalayhi wa sallam* said, 'Allah has more mercy for His servants than this women does for her child.'

I smiled. I remembered the story of the sufis who would not ask to be moved to the shade if they were under the sun. And I remembered the story I shared a few letters ago about Maarop Mohd Noh, who kissed the gravel that went into his shoes out of gratitude for Allah subhanahu wa taʻala.

Suddenly the sun did not seem so hot, and the gravel in my shoes wasn't that painful.

I reached campus only to find the classroom in darkness; class was cancelled. I turned on my heels, took a deep breath, smiled, and started the journey home again.

'If you are in love with Allah, you know that Allah will never do anything to upset you.'
—Shaykh Hamza Yusuf

Alhamdulillah.

May we always receive all that Allah subhanahu wa ta'ala gives to us with joy, understanding that He has more mercy for us than any creation could have for another, amin!

15

A Special Delivery from Palestine

Bismillah ir-Rahman ir-Rahim

'A friend of mine took twelve years to graduate from a bachelor's degree,' said the Palestinian student. He had been invited to the class to share his experiences of the conditions the Palestinians were living under.

The class gasped. 'Why?' Someone asked the question that was on everyone's mind.

'Because the Israelis would purposely coincide his jail time with his final examinations. So every time he was about to take his exams, they would take him into custody, and release him only when the exams were over. He had to keep repeating semester after semester just because of this.' The class became quiet with disbelief. The Palestinian student continued, 'and the sad thing was, the total time he was physically in jail was barely half a year. But it cost him more than a decade of his life!'

'Is this normal?'

'Unfortunately, yes,' said the Palestinian student, 'a lot of checkpoints are placed near universities to prevent students from getting an education. If they insist on going through the checkpoint when it is blocked, they get shot in the head.'

My lecturer stepped forward. 'When I was working with a non-profit organization, we faced many checkpoints too, but of a different kind. Once, we wanted to give the Palestinian doctors access to the latest medical knowledge and training, but the Israelis kept giving us one excuse or another, and did not allow us to bring in the books and tools we had brought with us. So in the end, we booked a hotel in Jordan, and shuttled the doctors there. Because they could not leave Palestine for more than twenty-four hours, as they risked being denied re-entry, and because they could not take the books into Palestine, the doctors would spend the day just pouring through the medical books. They committed every single thing to memory, just like that!'

'Yes,' the Palestinian student chimed in. 'Not only is it a struggle to seek knowledge, but it is a struggle to even impart knowledge. I know a professor who has two-thirds of his leg missing, and the soldiers would constantly make it hard for him to cross the checkpoints with his walking equipment. Sometimes he would end up going to university just by crawling, his shirt all brown from sand and soil. During times like these many professors cancelled their classes, but this professor? *Subhan Allah.*'

Someone raised his hand: 'It has been quite a long time that this is happening. Why can't everyone just stop fighting?'

'In Occupation,' explained the Palestinian student, 'you either fight, or you submit.'

'And we will never submit!' A shout rang out from the back of the class. I recognized the voice. It was my Syrian classmate. Three weeks ago she shared with me that her brothers might end up being citizen-less once their passports expire because they faced problems trying to renew them. She herself was not able to get an internship anywhere, because employees, even from Muslim countries, said it is 'policy' to not accept Syrians due to the current situation.

'But it has been dragging on for so long! Don't you feel tired? Isn't it all an exercise in futility?'

The Palestinian student smiled. It had been five years since he last saw his family. And it will probably be five to eight more years before he can return to his country, after his plans to complete his Masters and his PhD. His family said it will be too dangerous to return: 'Complete your education, and then come home to us.'

His nieces and nephews had all grown up without him. His friends had been thrown into jail, shot, or went missing. He talked to his family over Skype and wished he could hold them when they cry. But he is here, on the other side of the world, studying. So that he can do more and contribute to his family, his country, his religion.

'In the end, I know that Allah subhanahu wa ta'ala planned for this, and for all the things that we are going through. I know that the bigger plan of things, which only Allah knows, is good. So all I can do, all we can do, is to just do what we can, because Allah subhanahu wa ta'ala looks at our intentions and actions, and not the results.' The class was silent. I was silenced.

'This struggle you are going through brother, is a jihad by itself,' the Syrian girl quipped. The speakers crackled, and the *adhan* began across campus. The Palestinian student took a seat, and reflected on the conversation.

'Allahu akbar, Allahu akbar.' God is Greater. God is Greater.

May Allah subhanahu wa ta'ala protect and grant victory to our sisters and brothers in Syria, in Palestine, in Myanmar, in Yemen, and anywhere else around the world, amin.

16

How Changing Just One Thing in Your Life will Change Everything

Bismillah ir-Rahman ir-Rahim

Nothing in life happens by chance. Everything that happens to you, every single incident, every single moment, every single word or look someone gives to you, it all happens for one single purpose—to remind you of Allah subhanahu wa ta'ala. And in the reminders are lessons that He is trying to teach you. Allah subhanahu wa ta'ala is teaching you something. Hush. Listen.

In this letter, my lesson is about Intentions. An Intention is a very powerful thing; it is the very foundation of all our actions, and it determines not only the final outcome, but the emotions and thoughts we have when doing the action.

'When we are born, we are here to get it all from another. But when we die, there is nothing left to get; we give it all, unconditionally.'
—Shaykh Ebrahim Etsko Schuitema

All of us are on the highway to one destination: death. We will breathe in the air one last time, our eyes will close, never to open again, and our heart, which has been pumping roughly seventy-two beats a minute for our entire lifetime, will eventually fall silent.

Death is inevitable. You and I, we both know this. And yet some, upon the brink of death, struggle to let go, while others welcome death with open arms. The former group will face an ocean of uncertainty, of doubt and fear and a tightening of the chest so severe that the face is stricken with panic and doom, whilst the other group will step into the other world as if it is a homecoming. They both die, the outcome is the same. But one is unhappy, and the other is in bliss. Why? Because their intentions differ.

'Thus the process of maturation of our intent is the movement from one extreme to another—from getting it all, to giving it all.'
—Shaykh Ebrahim Etsko Schuitema

Think about it!

For several semesters, I struggled with other students getting hold of my notes and photocopying them without permission. I spent hours crafting them, and it felt unfair to have all my work distributed without my knowledge. I became upset when I saw my classmates smiling sheepishly when they were caught red-handed, and even more so when they blatantly flashed the papers around as if there wasn't a problem to begin with. When someone asked for help, I gave notes to them, and added, 'Don't pass them around, okay?' And yet they still did, and the notes were distributed and I became angry.

This semester it dawned upon me how selfish I had been. To battle my *nafs* (self), I did the opposite of what I had been doing before: I uploaded all the notes I made this semester onto a Dropbox file, and sent the link to the entire class. The next day, almost everyone I met had read the notes and used them to study for the test later that day. Some printed them out, others downloaded the notes to their smartphones. As in previous semesters, my notes were distributed, but this time I didn't get angry. In fact, I was happy; very happy. And so was everyone else.

I stopped thinking that by my classmates taking something from me, I would stand to lose something. Instead, by giving them something, both of us—myself especially—stood to benefit. When I changed my intent to one of giving—of serving—then the burden I felt on my chest was lifted. From doing housework, to sharing notes, to engaging in a required activity when I would rather be doing something else, it all works the same way. The one thing that changed everything was my intentions. And the power of intentions doesn't just stop there.

When Imam Abu Hanifa was on his deathbed he started making numerous intentions to do great things, like building a madrasah. His students asked him why he did so when he knew he didn't have long to live. The Imam replied: 'If I were to die, then Allah subhanahu wa ta'ala would give me the rewards for my intentions. If I were to live, then Allah subhanahu wa ta'ala would make these intentions a reality.' When a man built a madrasah, he made the intention that from that madrasah will rise someone who will free Palestine. Three hundred years later, Salahuddin al-Ayyubi went to that madrasah, and the rest, as they say, is history.

The Prophet *sallallahu 'alayhi wa sallam* said, 'Actions are according to intentions, and everyone will get what was intended.' If we truly reflect and understand that hadith, then we would consistently be renewing our intentions. Every single morning we wake up, we would ask ourselves, what do I intend for today? When we are about to perform a certain action, we would ask ourselves, what do I intend for this action? When we think about the future, when we plan the steps we wish to take, we would ask ourselves, what do I intend for my life? And when the dialogue in ourselves is that of constriction, of selfishness, and of wastefulness, we should look into ourselves, and ask what has gone wrong with my intentions?

Keeping to the right intentions is hard, but the struggle is the path and the path is to Allah. And Allah is teaching you every step of the way, guiding you in your struggle. So, hush. Listen. What is He teaching you today?

May Allah subhanahu wa ta'ala allow us the ability to silence our inner critic and hear His voice, and may He gift us the ability to make a thousand good intentions in all that we do and to renew them each time we forget, amin!

17

How We Overlook the Small things in Pursuit of the Grand

Bismillah ir-Rahman ir-Rahim

From my hostel window I watched as the cleaner dragged bags full of rubbish to the dumpster behind the building. Small and thin, she would take a deep breath before dragging a heavy black bag to the dumpster. Ten minutes later, she would return to the hostel, having dumped her first heavy load, then take another deep breath, grab another bag and repeat the same process. Back and forth, back and forth, until there were no more black bags lying on the ground. Then she'd take another deep breath, grab a broom, and start sweeping the corridors.

At the beginning of the semester, my course-mates and I came up with the idea of a campaign to raise awareness of the harsh conditions that the cleaners had to live and work in. Someone proposed we raise funds and organize an Appreciation Dinner. There would be good food, some (halal) entertainment, and gifts for them to take home. We were excited to show that we care. Except that the campaign wasn't approved, and everyone soon forgot about it (making me wonder how much we really cared in the first place).

Sometimes I try to come up with ideas on how I can help the cleaner servicing my hostel.

What can I do to improve her life substantially? Maybe I could design some posters and flyers reminding fellow students to minimize their environmental footprint? Maybe I could get everyone together to raise funds for the cleaners and help them out financially? Or maybe I could even set a day aside to help her carry out her cleaning duties!

I was having one of those thoughts when I saw a friend of mine, Hapsah, approaching the cleaner. She reached out for the cleaner's hand and kissed it, smiling and making conversation. Then I saw the cleaner reach for something from her bag. She dug around for a while, took out her uniform, and passed it to Hapsah. I was a little confused at first. Why did the cleaner pass Hapsah her uniform, did she need it for a class? Then I heard her say to the cleaner, 'Once I've ironed it, I will give it back to you.' *Subhan Allah.*

In trying to plan and organize something that was big and grand (and deliver a shot to my ego, I guess), I had completely overlooked the hadith of the Prophet *sallallahu 'alayhi wa sallam*: 'The most beloved of deeds to Allah are the most consistent of them, even if they are few.' Hapsah, on the other hand, understood the Sunnah well. Ironing the cleaner's uniform wasn't something 'big', but it was something she could do consistently, and it took one chore from the cleaner's daily grind. It made the cleaner happy, and it made her job easier. Meanwhile, my 'big' ideas remained as ideas, hampered by my own ego and excuses.

Allah ...

This week, let us take a lesson from Hapsah. Let us look around us, and find something small that we can do consistently to take a little pain from another person's burden. The person may be the resident cleaner at your apartment, or better still, perhaps someone from within your family (household chores, anyone?) May we always find lessons and inspirations from the people around us, and may we always be protected by Allah subhanahu wa ta'ala from our own nafs.

I pray that you have a blessed week ahead, and remember, let us try to start one consistent small act to take a small burden from someone around us. May our small deeds be multiplied with barakah. Amin!

18

How to Begin the New Year

Bismillah ir-Rahman ir-Rahim

It's a crisp sunny morning here in Gombak, Malaysia, where I'm currently residing. While millions around the world spent yesterday ushering in the new year with family and friends, I chose to sit by myself and reflect on how the last year had been for me, and to really think about how I want the next year to be.

Truth be told, I've never dedicated so much time to reflecting and making a real effort to see who I want to be in the coming years. There were two reasons I began my periods of reflection: Firstly, a lecture the previous year by Shaykh Hamza Yusuf stuck in my head, in which he explained the dangers of heedlessness. Basically, heedlessness means a lack of attentiveness, in this case, towards life itself. We go about our life just going through the motions, from one moment to the next, without really seeing the miracles, the lessons, the meanings of our life. We no longer take the time off to think, reflect, and give meaning, while too much time is plundered away doing things that are irrelevant to why we are here in this Dunya. The whole world today is designed to distract and to disrupt our deep thought. From the capitalist economy to the media industry, we have been programmed to follow order, to become cows slated for sacrifice, and unless we wake up and regain control of our lives by giving due attention to it, we're just like cattle. In fact, we're worse than cows because as the Qur'an says, we, unlike them, have intellect.

Secondly, I've been reading the book, *The Practice of Intent*, by Shaykh Ebrahim Schuitema, which was a perfect accompaniment to the talk by Shaykh Hamza. The book is a short read, at just twenty pages, but it gives solid advice that we can implement immediately in our daily life in order to 'pull out the minutiae of day-to-day events and to see things from an increasingly higher perspective.'[3]

One piece of advice I've taken and implemented successfully is that of daily journaling. Every morning, I wake up at 4 am, open my diary, and start writing about and reflecting on the previous day. True to what Shaykh Ebrahim says, it helps me to 'pull back further and further, in order to see the bigger picture'. Journaling is like having a conversation with myself and with Allah subhanahu wa ta'ala. I get to see myself from the perspective of the third person, taking into account my thoughts, emotions and actions. During one of the first few weeks of journaling, I was shocked to discover that for every

---

3.   Ebrahim Schuitema, *The Practice of Intent*, compiled by Saleem McGroarty (Edinburgh: Intent Publishing, 2012) http://www.lulu.com/shop/etsko-schuitema/the-practice-of-intent/ebook/product-20243686.html accessed on 24 September 2018.

single day of the week, I had allowed my short temper to get the better of me. I'm more conscious of my temper today, and though I still have moments where I am on a short fuse, I feel a lot better, *Alhamdulillah*. So between really understanding why heedlessness is the greatest danger of our time, to making the conscious effort to overcome heedlessness, spending a whole day reflecting and making new intentions seemed like a natural thing to do after all the journaling I've been doing. *Alhamdulillah*.

I hope you will take some time off today, or at the weekend, from everything and everyone, and watch the lecture by Shaykh Hamza,[4] and read the free ebook by Shaykh Ebrahim. Then, start spending some time with Allah subhanahu wa ta'ala and yourself. Have conversations with yourself, be raw and truthful, dig deep and reach high. No one is around to judge you, so be honest to yourself. Forgive and let go of the past, accept what is, and renew or make better intentions for the future.

May Allah subhanahu wa ta'ala grant us a good beginning, and a good end, *insha' Allah*. Amin.

4.　Hamza Yusuf, *The Dangers of Heedlessness* (Zaytuna Institute, 2007), video recording, YouTube <https://www.youtube.com/watch?v=1ejQXZdh-Z4> viewed 24 September 2018.

19

What to Avoid When Calling Friends and Family to Islam

Bismillah ir-Rahman ir-Rahim

My brothers and I fought a lot when I first returned to Islam. In my new-found zeal in rediscovering my *din*, and my misplaced illusion that I knew everything on earth after attending several classes, I went full throttle on them with the preaching: 'Why are you wearing this? It's haram!' I would say. 'XYZ are bad influences, you should leave them!' and 'Why aren't you praying? It's sinful!'

It never occurred to me that I wasn't in the right place to lecture them about any of the things I was telling them! Since I had entered adolescence, I was seldom around and I barely saw them. I would go to school in the morning, head to town in the evening, and come home late at night, heading straight to my room. We spoke as little as we could, barely had any real conversations, and the only times we didn't fight were when we head-banged in the living room listening to some Punk rock, Emo-core or Ska music I wanted to share (or when I grabbed my electric guitar and we pretended I could actually play that sexy thing).

It was probably a shock to them when I did a complete 180-degree turn, took down all the CDs and posters covering my walls, and started backtracking on all the insane nonsense I had shared with them. I was convinced that I had led them astray, and was trying to get them to follow my new path instead. Almost every single day they were greeted at home by a sister who was trying to persuade them to attend a class, or to pray on time, or to start reading the Qur'an. Every. Single. Day. Until one day, one of my brothers snapped.

We were happily having lunch as a family when he started sharing how an irritable neighbour had called the police on him and his friends when they were repairing their bikes. He was laughing whilst sharing the story (because they really didn't do anything wrong), but me, being 'Preachy' Fadhilah, began to lecture him on how we should be good to our neighbours and be considerate, and the importance of having good friends. Barely a minute into my lecture, my brother stood up, threw some magazine he wanted to share onto the floor, shouted something at me (I was too shocked to register), and stormed off. A cold war settled over the house for the next few days. We would avoid eye-contact, not eat together, and avoid even being in the same space together.

And then my holidays were over, and I had to return to campus. I packed my luggage, peeked into the room where he was sleeping, and boarded the bus to Kuala Lumpur in the wee hours of the morning without saying goodbye. Five hours later, I was awoken at my destination by my phone vibrating in my pocket. I took it out and was surprised to see a Facebook message from my brother. It read (and I summarize and paraphrase): 'I think I know the feeling of what it's like to want to say sorry to someone but never get the chance to do so. But I'm lucky you've only gone to Kuala Lumpur, and not gone forever. I'm sorry, sis.' I cried, because I knew the one who could learn a lesson was me, not him. He was the first to apologize, he was the first to admit a mistake, and I was still placing myself on a pedestal that I was 'right' and deserved an apology from him.

Over the next few days we began exchanging messages. He shared with me how hard it was for him to accept my drastic change, how every time I preached it made him angry with himself for not being able to fully embrace Truth. It was hard, day in and day out, to live with the new me who was trying to force my ideals onto everyone in the house. In those conversations, we began to start bonding, and soon the topics expanded to just about everything under the sun. I stopped preaching, and I started listening. I began to know him as a person, to understand the problems and struggles he had, and I really learned to love him as he is. When I returned to Singapore for the holidays, we (along with my other brother) would make an effort to go out and spend time together, something we have never done, ever.

In all the time we spent together talking, I rarely spoke about Islam. All I concentrated on was just being a good sister, by being there, being as non-judgmental as I could and upholding my new values. And then slowly, over time, the questions about Islam started coming in. I answered as best I could, without imposing, and when I did not know how to answer, I directed them to someone who could. Today, *Alhamdulillah*, my brother makes his own effort to attend classes, listens to Islamic lectures, draws beautiful *khat* (Arabic calligraphy) that people actually want to buy, and is starting to learn Arabic. All without my preaching and nagging. You see, the first step to making *da'wah* is love, not self-righteousness or the want to 'save' others.

Shaykh Abdul Aziz Fredericks ate pizzas with gangsters in Denmark for weeks, talking about nothing but football and rock music, until they started asking him about Islam. After a few months, crimes related to gangsters dropped, the prostitutes around the area started wearing the hijab and attending classes, and the priest from the church in the area loved it so much he offered to pay for all future pizzas to help spread Islam.

Another Shaykh (can't remember who) shared that if you want your family and friends to start knowing Islam, then start by spending time with them and inculcating love between you. If they like to talk about Justin Bieber, then talk about Justin Bieber. If they like soccer, start playing soccer with them. The more time you spend together, the more love you have for one another, the more they will think about you and your ideals, and *insha' Allah* one day they will start asking questions.

What we should first do is to love, to build real solid relationships, to make lots of du'a', and to always act as the Prophet *sallallahu 'alayhi wa sallam* has told us to. It may take a day. It may take months. It might even take years. But in the end, guidance is from Allah. Not from you, and definitely not from me.

May Allah subhanahu wa ta'ala keep our hearts on the *din*, open the hearts of our family and friends to His guidance, and may He keep us *istiqamah* (consistent) on all the changes we want to inculcate in our lives. Amin!

20

Understanding Love

Bismillah ir-Rahman ir-Rahim

It was close to ten at night when the tear of cold water sliding down my cheek woke me from a heavy slumber. I was feverish and still weak from having lost so much fluid earlier in the day, and the injection and medication prescribed by the doctor had only added to the fog in my head. My eyes flickered open. My friend, Nazra, sat quietly on the bed, wringing water from a soaked towel before placing it gently on my forehead.

I smiled and struggled to sit up. She glared at me with a 'don't you dare' expression and gently pushed me back down. The damp towel felt heavenly; I closed my eyes and allowed myself the pleasure of imagining my fever being lifted into the heavens along with my sins. Nazra tugged at the sides of the blanket covering me, making sure I was warm. The bed creaked as she got up and I opened my eyes and saw her tidying the stuff on the floor, forgotten and ignored in the panic when she and Sajaf had hurriedly sent me to the doctor's just hours before. I watched as she moved around silently, and suddenly remembered all of the stained blankets, sheets, clothes and pillowcases. 'Nazra,' my voice croaked, 'my sheets?' She walked over and sat next to me.

'I've washed them for you, don't worry.'

'And Sajaf? Has she started studying for her paper tomorrow morning?'

'She's studying now, don't worry about her. We just want you to get well. We're worried.'

I felt a lump rising at the back of my throat, and tears begin to well in my eyes. Nazra had barely slept the night before studying for a paper, and Sajaf had a paper to prepare for the next morning. And yet on that day, both of them sacrificed their time and energy rushing me to the doctor, cleaning up after the huge mess I had made, and had taken turns to check on me as I slept, slowly recovering.

'How do you and Sajaf do it? I don't understand how both of you can give and love so sincerely to everyone around you—family, friends, and strangers alike. I want to love endlessly and sincerely like the both of you, but I feel like I don't understand love, no matter how many books I read. I can talk about it, sure, but I feel like I don't understand it the way you and Sajaf do.' I choked, revealing in my moment of weakness a burden I had been carrying in my chest for months. 'Why am I not able to understand love the way you and Sajaf do?'

I looked at Nazra, pleading for an answer to the question that had finally escaped from the depths of my heart and released itself into the space between us. She smiled kindly before answering, wiping away the hot tears that rolled down my cheeks: 'Love is not something which you can understand with your mind, Fadhilah. It is something that can only be understood when you search with your heart.'

Allah ...

I closed my eyes and let the night carry her words into my soul.

May Allah subhanahu wa ta'ala allow us the gift of understanding what True Love is, to be someone who is capable of giving and receiving it, and may He make us beloved to all those beloved to Him, amin.

21

Giving Everyting Its Due

Bismillah ir-Rahman ir-Rahim

The train rumbled onwards, its wheels screeching, struggling to move as it carried the heavy load on its back. Every few minutes it would stop to regurgitate some of its contents, only to be filled up with more each time. At every station, I found myself wondering if trains have a maximum load. Could one burst at the seams? Would the tracks give way under the sheer weight of the train and its increasing number of passengers? What is the possibility of a seemingly infinite number of passengers dying from suffocation?

Beads of sweat clustered on my forehead. It was hot, but at least I had a seat. I clutched the pole next to me as the train lurched forward, throwing several commuters off balance and into the arms of their neighbours. Embarrassed smiles and hushed apologies, a tight-lipped nod of understanding; we are all in this together. The train soon rolled to a stop and the destination, 'KL Sentral,' echoed around the carriage. The doors whooshed open, letting in much needed ventilation, and I watched with faint nonchalance as the mad scramble began once again; bruised shoulders, tripped feet, and the deep intake of air (depending if you're getting on or getting off). 'Doors are closing.' The train moved on towards its next stop.

A battered vintage suitcase caught my eye. It wasn't there a moment ago, someone must have just boarded. I looked up to see a confused-looking man, his face tired and his posture weary, clutching the suitcase with both hands whilst trying to hold his balance. It looked difficult. My first instinct was to stand and give up my seat to him. But I didn't. Still embedded in my seat, my mind began an inner dialogue: 'He's a man. You're a woman. Don't you need the seat more than him? And if you get up for him, what would that Chinese man standing at the corner from just now think? That you are racist and would help only Malay-Muslims? That would reflect badly on you wouldn't it? No, it will reflect badly on all Malay-Muslims! Yes, I know you feel bad that he's struggling to stand, but you too have that heavy bag to carry. If you stand up, you would totally block the other passengers, and …'. The lady next to me stood up and the man with the suitcase sat, looking extremely relieved and eternally grateful. He communicated his thanks, and she looked genuinely happy to have been able to help. I sat between them, disappointed with myself for having lost the opportunity to do good.

'Every moment Allah presents something
and we are to give its due courtesy.'
—Shaykh Ebrahim Schuitema

In the weary man's presence was a potential transaction, a hidden catalyst towards a person's growth. He was presented equally to all those around him, an opportunity for those alert and mindful enough to see him as what he is supposed to be—a present from Allah subhanahu wa ta'ala. The lady who stood up recognized the opportunity, and she responded accordingly by giving the situation its due. I, on the other hand, had allowed my needs and my wants to cloud my judgments and actions, and in my sense of self-justification had denied myself a gift that was made available to me in that moment.

For the rest of the journey, I sat with a heavy heart. The blessing of having a seat no longer felt like a blessing, but instead felt like a prison sentence I had to endure. At every station I looked for reasons to give up my seat, and when I finally found a person who needed one, I stood up without question and took my rightful place on the floor alongside the other commuters. But I did not feel happy, nor did the giving feel like a gift. Because the original moment—that gift from Allah—had passed me by, and all I had was regret.

'... if you confront the situation on the basis of what you want to get from it, it defines you and you get stuck.'
—Shaykh Ebrahim Schuitema

May Allah subhanahu wa ta'ala enable us to give every situation its due courtesy, and to see His gifts for what they are.

22

Why I Stopped Shoving My Beliefs down Others' Throats

Bismillah ir-Rahman ir-Rahim

I used to get so worked up about different causes. Like *really* worked up. Like crazy-lady-with-laser-eyes worked up. Piu, piu, piu!

When I first found out about the atrocities happening in Palestine, I spent days just reading and researching, falling ill because of the knots that were tightening in my heart. How could this happen? Why isn't the Muslim world doing anything about it? I came across the Boycott, Divestment and Sanctions (BDS) movement, and I began striking brand after brand off my list: Starbucks, McDonalds, Nestlé. Out, out, out! Then I set out to get everyone involved. I remember walking around town with my cousin when we passed by Starbucks. Her eyes turned glassy and she stopped in her tracks, scanning the menu in the window. I squirmed, feeling my heart pounding in my chest. 'Babe, a percentage of the proceeds from Starbucks goes to the Israeli army, you know.'

'Uhuh … Should I get Mocha or Javachip?'

'Did you hear what I said? When you buy Starbucks, you are supporting the genocide happening in Israel!'

'Javachip it is,' my cousin grinned, eyes wide open, giving me the 'Why should I care?' look. Five minutes later she bounced out of the café, a cup of Javachip in hand. It used to be my favourite drink.

'Every sip you're drinking is a bullet through a Palestinian child's head,' I mocked, both furious and disappointed by her devil-may-care attitude. She stopped walking, turned to face me, and made a long deliberate slurp, 'Mmm … This coffee is sooooooo delicious!' I wanted to shoot a bullet through her head.

Fast-forward a year later, I was facing an audience of forty, including a lecturer I highly respected. I had just concluded a fifteen-minute presentation on the Dinar and Dirham movement, ending with a strong call for those in the class to change their existing ideas about fiat money. It was one of my best presentations; I was on a roll! I turned off the slides, 'Any questions?' The dirham coin I had brought to the class was passed around and was now in my lecturer's hands, and I watched as he inspected it against the light. The coin was a beauty—a simple circle with an image of the Ka'bah engraved in the centre.

The class was quiet, but I could see the students' minds just buzzing with thoughts. A hand surfaced from the back of the class. 'Yes?'

'You mentioned that the banking system is essentially haram, and the right way to go is by returning to the dinar and dirham. But what about the Islamic banking system? Why can't we just use that?'

I had anticipated that question; it was one of the first things I asked when I began my own journey learning about Islamic finance. My mind began scanning through the different texts I read. Brrrr ... kerching! Found it.

'One of the shaykhs supporting the movement says this: Islamic banking, even though it contains the word Islam, is just as guilty of *riba* (usury/interest rates) as the conventional banks. If you build a musollah inside a brothel, that doesn't make the brothel Islamic, right?'

The answer sucked the air out of the room. It hung there, hovering in the space between the ears, unsure of where to go. My lecturer raised his eyebrows. I couldn't figure out if he was angry or amused. He walked to the front of the class, motioning me to take a seat. Once again facing the students, he looked at me directly in the eye, and said, 'You are still a student. Learn to learn, and learning means to be objective, not to be fanatic. There is a lot of *khilaf* (differences in opinion) about this matter, so perhaps you should read more before quoting a statement like that to the class.'

I still got an A for the presentation, but I felt like I deserved a C. I've learned that there are two ways of sharing your beliefs. The first is to shove your truth down others' throats and force them to swallow it, whether they like it or not, or whether they are ready for it or not. The second is to lay out your truth, and leave it to others to make the decision of whether to accept it. A shaykh once said: 'The word *da'wah* means to invite. When you invite someone to your home, you don't kidnap him and force him to drink your tea.' Also, I use the phrase 'your truth' because unless something is black and white, clear cut halal and haram as agreed by all the scholars, then it is not *the* truth, but your truth. It means scholars have differing opinions about it, so accept that different people can carry different opinions. Your truth may be the truth, their truth may be the truth, both of your truths may be the truth, *wallahua'lam*.

The Prophet *sallallahu 'alayhi wa sallam* said in a hadith that differences in opinion in his Ummah are a blessing. When a mujtahid (a learned scholar who is allowed to call a ruling) makes a judgment and he gets it right, he gets two rewards. If another mujtahid makes a judgment and he gets it wrong, he doesn't sin; he still gets one reward.

I stopped shoving my beliefs down the throats of others, because in doing so I insinuate that my truth is the only truth, and I tend to get all emotional and judgmental when others don't respond. When I shove, I am committing an act of aggression, of hostility. I am coming from an elevated opinion of my own thoughts and beliefs. I am assuming that I am right and you are wrong. Instead, I should begin by laying down what I know, and leave it to others to accept. And then I make du'a' for Allah to guide me if I'm wrong, and for Allah to guide them if they are wrong. I am still a student, I am not a mujtahid.

Several months ago I walked past Starbucks with the same cousin I wanted to shoot in the head. I saw her looking in, and asked if she wanted to stop and get some coffee. She continued walking, saying, 'Nah, I read that they are supporting Israel.' She turned to me and curled her fingers into a mock pistol. 'Piuuuuu!' I just got shot in the head.

May Allah subhanahu wa ta'ala gift us with wisdom in *da'wah*, amin.

***

Author's note, three years later: To further prove the above point about differences in opinion, today I no longer believe in the Dinar and Dirham movement I used to preach about, after further reading on the matter coupled with developments in events. This does not mean that the movement is wrong (*wallahu a'lam*). It just means my standing on it has changed. May Allah subhanahu wa ta'ala guide us to what is right, and bring us away from falsehood, amin!

23

What Happens When You are Grateful?

Bismillah ir-Rahman ir-Rahim

I've been worrying a lot the past month or so, thinking of ways in which I can raise funds to pay for my final semester. While my mind was constantly buzzing with ideas, my heart was constantly laden with negative thoughts—the many what-ifs and alternative futures that could happen should the target amount fail to be achieved.

For weeks, I would spend my mornings brainstorming ideas, then spend the rest of the time researching, planning and putting together those ideas. When I finally launched several of them, like the *Making Resolutions Work* ebook or the Web Development Service, I would spend more hours fretting over the prospect of failure. And for what little time I had left, I would write different proposals to different organizations, in hope of securing a part-time remote job.

Needless to say, my inner dialogue was one that was constantly filled with noise. I was always in a state of insecurity; my chest was heavy, my breath shallow, and my heart was wound tight. I was submerged in an ocean of worry and stress, and I had lost sight of the clear skies above. *Until He found me and guided me.* Only then, could I finally breathe.

It was Saturday morning, and my mother and I were at the local *masjid* listening to the ustadh's (religious teacher) sermon. Knowing the poor state of my heart, I made a silent prayer for Him to help me get out of the anxiety-filled state I was in; I was beyond exhausted living the way I did. 'Amin,' I whispered, looking up at the ustadh. I wanted so badly for Allah subhanahu wa ta'ala to make the ustadh His spiritual catalyst to get my message across. I needed something, anything, to bring me to the surface again. I was desperate for air. Barely seconds later, the ustadh recited a verse of the Qur'an that I knew all too well, but seemed to have forgotten: *'And remember when your Lord proclaimed, "If you are grateful, I will surely increase you in favour; but if you deny, indeed, My punishment is severe."'* (Ibrahim 14: 7)

I don't know how I finally saw it, but it dawned on me that the state of anxiety I was in was a result of the careless ingratitude I had towards the blessings given by Allah subhanahu wa ta'ala; this was His punishment! I was ungrateful, and because of that, I was made to walk around in a state of living, but not alive. Shocked, I began weeping, thinking of all the blessings He had given me since I started my degree. I sobbed in total thankfulness, recalling the times He had given me enough *rizq* (sustenance) to pay for my tuition fees through His spiritual catalysts—from people who were close to me, people who barely knew me, and those who didn't even know me at all.

I hung my head in shame for forgetting that every single time I came home, He surrounded me with family and friends who are always quick to foot the bill and pitch in towards my expenses: 'When you start work again, it'll be your turn to treat us!' I had all of these blessings and more, much more, and yet I had the cheek to forget and instead, lose my mind thinking that I was in charge of my own *rizq*.

Allah, Allah ...

I spent the rest of that Saturday with my family, finally free from the shackles of financial worry and entirely present with my heart and soul. I spent the day in the kitchen, preparing and packing food with my mother, joking around with cousins I had not met for months, and walking around with '*Alhamdulillah*' pounding against my chest.

That night before I went to bed, my mind was clear and my chest was light. As I was about to doze off, my phone beeped. I reached for it, and the message, from a person I had not spoken to in months, said: 'Use the money for your school fees ok?' Surprised, I checked my accounts. An amount the total of a quarter of my school fees was just sitting there, without me even expecting it to come from anyone, at any time.

'And which of the blessings of your Lord shall you deny?'
(*al-Rahman* 55: 13)

Allah, Allah ...

May Allah subhanahu wa ta'ala remind us that He is Al-Razzaq (The Provider), and may He increase us in *rizq* that will be beneficial to us in this world and the next. May He make us one of His thankful slaves, and may we always be in a state of remembrance, *insha' Allah*, amin!

24

What are We Praying For?

Bismillah ir-Rahman ir-Rahim

Over the weekend, my friends and I explored an area of the city we've never been before. Out of curiosity, we entered the place of worship of another religion; it was barely 10 am, yet the place was already buzzing with activity—from adults immersed in prayer, faces scrunched and determined, to children running around as they met cousins and friends. My friends and I stood in the centre of the building, taking photos and sticking out like sore thumbs in our hijab and with our clearly tourist-like body language. As the place became more crowded, we were slowly pushed into a corner, where we bumped into a man selling offerings.

'Hi! Could you explain to us how you pray?' A friend asked, hands gesturing towards the main prayer hall. The rest of us huddled closer, turning our ears to the shopkeeper in hopes of capturing his reply amid the din.

'Sure,' he smiled, his hands swiftly pocketing the wad of cash a customer had just handed him. 'That,' his finger pointed at the smallest idol out of three, 'that is the god of health. So if any of us are sick, we go to him and pray to get well.' We nodded. 'And that,' this time his finger moved to the idol sitting on the extreme left; small, but bigger than the god of health, 'that is the god of lineage. When a couple is unable to get a child, we go to him to ask for one.'

'How about the one in the centre? The biggest of them all?' Another friend asked, gesturing at the gigantic idol in the centre of the hall, attracting the largest crowd.

'That,' the shopkeeper beamed, 'is the god of wealth. If we want our job and business to succeed, if we want to get more money, we ask it from him. We even have a special area behind you where we can give more offerings to get even wealthier!'

As if on cue, a man hustled past us, mumbling some chants, before depositing his offerings—a huge bag of offerings—into the special area. We watched as the offerings disappeared before turning back to our impromptu guide, only to find his back turned as he tended to his customers. My friends and I made for the exit in silence.

'Correct me if I'm wrong, but would it be right to say that the size and prominence of each idol represents his importance in the worldview of his worshippers?' Nazra spoke up as soon as we were a reasonable distance away. 'If that's true, then the foremost worry of the worshippers would be the things of this Dunya—accruing wealth!'

'I might be wrong too, but I get the feeling that the foundation of their religion is based on transactions,' I added my two cents worth as I watched more families making their way towards the place of worship. 'That is, I give god my prayers and offerings in order to get something from god, be it health, children or wealth. It's not worshipping god for god himself, but to get something from god. So who's actually the god?'

There was a moment of silence as we continued down an alley flanked on either side by beautiful shops. Elderly men and women were slowly moving around in their stores, arranging their wares for the day ahead. Suddenly Sajaf piped up, her face released from the frown it had been scrunched into as she found the words to her thoughts: 'I'm just thankful that I don't have to buy offerings when I want or need to pray. I'm thankful that Allah subhanahu wa ta'ala listens to each and every one of us without looking at what we can offer Him.'

'Alhamdulillah,' we chorused, smiling to ourselves.

Later that night, as I sat on my prayer mat making du'a' for good health and rizq, it dawned on me that perhaps, in the subtlest of ways, I too was guilty of that of which I spoke. What are my du'a's filled with? My worries for this world or my longing for Him and His Beloved? What are my thoughts preoccupied with? How to make more in order to get by in this world day by day, or how to prepare myself to meet Him when there are no more days left? And do I only crawl to Him when I need something? Do I only wake up in the middle of the night to be with Him when the trials of this Dunya are becoming too much to bear? Do I earnestly raise my hands only when I want to get something—a promotion, better grades, a spouse?

Am I worshipping Allah subhanahu wa ta'ala for Allah, or am I worshipping Him to get something out of it? I closed my eyes, and the room fell away.

I thank Allah subhanahu wa ta'ala for accepting me, even as I'm lacking in every way. May we learn to worship Allah subhanahu wa ta'ala as He deserves to be worshipped, amin!

25

Slow Down, Stand Still, Experience

Bismillah ir-Rahman ir-Rahim

I found myself standing still, just looking towards the horizon. Everyone around me was silent, enjoying the scene that unfolded before us—majestic mountains in various hues pushing towards the skies and paddy fields coloured a luscious green, swaying and bending to the tune of the wind. The occasional flock of birds danced in the air, soaring and dipping. A lone scarecrow peered at them, and at us, a group of visitors from the city in the quaint little village that is Kampung Lonek.

It had been some time since I last felt this sense of peace, this feeling of stillness. I closed my eyes, breathing in the cold air and feeling the breeze embrace my skin. Though no one would see it, I smiled all the same; a smile emanating from within my core, a smile that I could no longer contain inside. After what had been a tremendously busy and exhausting week, the time at the village—slow and still—was something I desperately craved. No worries of deadlines tugging the back of my mind, no running through systems, figures, and flows, no planning or brainstorming of any kind. Just quiet.

A peaceful, serene, quiet that blanketed all the noise in the world ... all the noise in my mind. My heart lifted and I felt its beat resonate to the tip of my fingers. I felt the air enter my nose and fill my lungs, before spreading to the tip of my toes. In the presence of such beauty created by Allah subhanahu wa ta'ala, even the trail of my voice vanished into thin air, leaving only a barely audible hum of *dhikr*: *Subhan Allah. Alhamdulillah. Allahu akbar.*

In our race towards efficiency and productivity, we constantly find ourselves accelerating, running forward, and pushing our boundaries. How can we do more in a shorter period of time? How can we maximize our time and fill it with activities full of goodness? How do we fulfil a rainbow of responsibilities with only twenty-four hours in a day? As we find ourselves on board the bullet train, we forget to step off at each station to experience the beauty that is life. So intent are we on making the best of the journey that we forget to experience the journey itself. We are so used to the blur of the scenery as it passes us by that we do not know how to appreciate life. The Prophet *sallallahu 'alayhi wa sallam* was a shepherd, and yet he always took time to retreat to the mountains and caves to dedicate his time for reflection.

When was the last time we let our mind be silent? When was the last time we reflected on our emotions, thoughts, and actions? When was the last time we coaxed our heart, mind, and *nafs* to be quiet, and instead reach out and listen to what Allah subhanahu wa ta'ala is telling us? So busy are we in trying to make the best out of our life that perhaps we have forgotten what it's like to truly live:

> An explorer, a white man, anxious to reach his destination in the heart of Africa, promised an extra payment to his bearers if they would make greater speed. For several days, the bearers moved along at a faster pace.
>
> One afternoon, though, they all suddenly put down their burden and sat on the ground. No matter how much money they were offered, they refused to move on. When the explorer finally asked why they were behaving as they were, he was given the following answer: 'We have been moving along at such a fast pace that we no longer know what we are doing. Now we have to wait until our soul catches up with us.'
> —An excerpt from *Maktub*, by Paulo Coelho

So slow down. Be still. Watch your mother's chest rise and fall as she sleeps; the lines on her face are more pronounced than they were yesterday. Feel the soft skin of your child's fingers as he pulls at you, wanting to connect. Listen to the voice of your soul as it struggles to share with you the secrets of your Rabb.

May we return to our Rabb with our souls at rest, amin.

26

Sculpting the Self

Bismillah ir-Rahman ir-Rahim

These past few weeks have been nothing but a blur. Those of you who have added me on Facebook have probably noticed my cry for help in trying to cope with being appointed head of the university's news team. For days I lived like a duck in water—calm above the surface, but with legs paddling like mad underwater, trying to keep afloat.

One particular morning, after spending a number of days bent over my laptop scrambling for news and editing articles before Fajr (dawn prayer), I broke down and began to cry. I couldn't deal with the change. I hated the fact that my precious morning hours spent with Him and for self-reflection were being used for getting up to speed with events on campus and terrorist bombings on the other side of the world. I resented that those hours I used to spend writing and making a difference to myself and others were now taken over by the task of writing articles that would be out of date just hours after being published. I was angry that I had allowed my clear morning mind to be cluttered and jammed with worldly events.

Every single day, I would wake up and stare begrudgingly at the laptop on my desk and feel a sense of dread wash over me. Why am I doing this? How does doing this matter in any way? Why did I agree to take on this position? I was angry at myself and full of regret. And so, that particular morning, exhausted and drained, I began to cry. I couldn't understand why I was being made to go through this. I was in denial. I was resisting. I was constantly thinking that my entire semester, my final four months in the university, would be ruined. I was going to be ruined. In tears, my exhausted heart cried out: 'Ya Allah, show me, Ya Allah! Show me!' In truth, I doubted that He would answer, for my heart was dark and heavy and I felt so far away from Him; it had been days since I last spent time in His company. But He did answer me. He always does.

Later in the day, I decided on a whim to re-read one of my favourite books, *The Millennium Discourses*, by Shaykh Ebrahim Etsko Schuitema. Flipping to a random page, I was in tears again as my eyes touched upon the first paragraph:

> When you rise to whatever He has given you in the moment, you allow Him to chisel you. You accept the blows that He is giving you because you realise that the blow is about you becoming yourself. You do not complain about the hardness of the blow because you recognise that it is for you. It enables you to become,

to appear, like a sculpture coming out of stone. Sir Henry Moore once said that when he sculpts a horse he takes away all the rock that does not look like a horse.

This is what Allah does with us. He calls us out of undifferentiated existence by impacting on us with events. The events are His hammer and His chisel. With these He gives us our shape and our form.

Just like that, my inner wall of resentment and resistance began to crack, and rays of light began to fall onto the situation I found myself in. I began to see again, recognizing the moment for what it was meant to be, understanding the meaning behind the events that unfold in my life. I was in the process of being chiselled by Allah subhanahu wa ta'ala. I was in the process of becoming myself.

In my denial, I was blind to the fact that the experience had taught me so much about myself and about being a leader. In my resistance, I refused to see how the experience made me much better in dealing with different kinds of people. In getting caught up with my anger and anxiety, I missed the valuable lessons of patience, of *rida* (being well-pleased and content with what Allah decrees),[5] and of *tawakkul* (putting one's trust and reliance in Allah) that I could have attained.

The fact is that a lot of us tend to do the same thing, over and again, in our lives: we resist. When something beyond our control happens—getting laid off work, failing at something after trying so damn hard at it, losing someone—our first reaction is to resist the moment and fight against it. We get confused, we get angry, we

---

5.   Aisha Bewley, *The Glossary of Islamic Terms* (London: Ta-Ha, 1988), p. 69.

question why Allah subhanahu wa ta'ala placed us in that position. Why are we made to go through so much pain?

When we focus too much on our pain and negative emotions, we lose sight of the good that is in that situation (and there is always inherent good in every situation). When we don't actively seek out the wisdom behind things that happen, we are in actuality denying that He wishes only the best for us. When we choose to notice only the pain brought by the hammer, we will never see the beautiful sculpture coming from within us.

May Allah subhanahu wa ta'ala give us the gift of remembrance and patience, and may He allow us to see the wisdom behind all things, amin!

27

A Moment of Gratitude

Bismillah ir-Rahman ir-Rahim

There are always things to be grateful for, if you choose to adopt an attitude of gratitude. It's been a tough week here in Malaysia; a heatwave has descended and the skies are choked by the haze; water levels are depleting, with several areas having to go through water rationing exercises; and recent news of the missing airplane, MH370, has sent the country into mourning.

In the midst of trials and tribulations, it's easy to get worked up and forget the blessings that we do have. For most of us living in developed countries, it's easy to complain about the smallest of inconveniences, while disregarding the vast amount of blessings Allah subhanahu wa ta'ala has granted us. The blessings of peace in our country, the blessings of being able to worship Him subhanahu wa ta'ala, the blessings of each and every breath of life.

While Muslims around the world are raped and tortured as slaves, brutally murdered in ethnic genocides, or starving from the lack of food in refugee camps, we are here, at this moment, having the luxury of reading this letter of mine. How pale are our inconveniences compared to what our sisters and brothers are facing? When I was younger, I used to scoff when my mother scolded me for not finishing up my food. As with most Asian mothers, she would end her lecture with: 'Finish your food. The people in Africa don't even have anything to eat.' To the younger me, this was flawed logic—whether or not I finished my food does not affect the stomach of Africans. Today, I know better. Perhaps, the simple lesson my mother was trying to teach me was not one of demand, supply, or the international food trade, but the lesson of being grateful and of counting my blessings.

Let us take a moment from our rambling inner voice to count our blessings. When we lie in bed at night ready for sleep, let us allow the last thoughts in our mind to be that of gratitude, of *shukr*. When we wake up in the early morning, let us allow the first thought to cross our mind to be that of gratitude for being granted one more day to return to Him. Abu Yahya Suhayb ibn Sinan *radhiallahu 'anhu* reported that the Messenger of Allah *sallallahu 'alayhi wa sallam* said: 'How wonderful is the case of a believer; there is good for him in everything and this applies only to a believer. If prosperity befalls him, he expresses gratitude to Allah and that is good for him; and if adversity befalls him, he endures it patiently and that is good for him.' (*Sahih* Muslim) *Alhamdulillah. Alhamdulillah* for everything.

May we always be grateful for each blessing that He bestows upon us because the blessing of a single eye cannot even be paid by a thousand years of worship! Amin!

28

Make a Difference

Bismillah ir-Rahman ir-Rahim

Many among us would like to make a difference to the world. Even as we live our average lives, running the rat race, we silently dream about doing something that will change the world for the better, if not, change our lives for the better. But the problem with most of us is that we remain stuck in that stage—the dreaming stage. Afraid of the work, challenges, and risks that need to be undertaken if we pursue our dreams, we settle, and we begin to sabotage our work before it has even begun. The most common thing we—I—say to ourselves is: 'How can I make such a difference? I am only an average person. I am neither a genius, nor a wealthy person, nor was I raised in the upper crust of society. I grew up getting average grades and doing normal things. Other people may be destined for greatness, but not me. I am destined to be average.'

When we tell ourselves that we cannot make a difference, that we are too small and average, then why should we be surprised or disappointed when we do end up being average? Our thoughts are a self-fulfilling prophecy of the things that come into our lives. We need to stop sabotaging ourselves, and begin to pursue our dreams. We need to just *do*. I once read a quote from Buddha, which I printed and stuck to my wall: 'Our thoughts make our actions. And our actions make our world.' Let me share with you today a true story of one of the readers of these letters I deliver each week. Yes, a reader, just like you. The story goes like this ...

In every family there is a black sheep, and where I'm studying, the English Department has always been regarded by the rest of the student body as the black sheep of the otherwise Islamic university. Due to their deep engagement with Western culture and literature, students of the department were regularly branded with words like 'liberal', 'modern', and 'Western-wannabes.' It is so bad that when someone acts a little outside of the Islamic norms, all it usually takes to reason why is to mention that '(so-and-so) is from the English Department!'

However, I noticed this semester that the student club of the English Department had been slowly, but regularly, organizing talks and programmes that were—you guessed it—Islamic. With titles like the 'Literature as a Tool for *Da'wah*' and 'Islamisation of Human Knowledge', I found myself wondering what had happened to the club? Have they gone mad? Were they directed by the powers-to-be to clean up their act? It was all a mystery to me until I met the reader I mentioned. And then everything made sense.

Born into a typically normal family, this reader—let's call her Latifah—spent her youth doing average things like jamming with her siblings, going to the mall, and engaging in ordinary teenage activities. She was neither too religious nor too 'intellectual'. In short, she was, by general standards, 'normal'—just like you and me. When we first met, it was to discuss some work I had proposed we do together. But when we got to really talking, I discovered that Latifah, normal, average Latifah, had recently been elected to help lead the student club of the English Department. With the 'little' power she had in her position, she chose to push forward an Islamic agenda for the club, simultaneously changing the value that the club offers to the university, while at the same time clearing away years' worth of bad reputation and notoriety.

Latifah could have allowed her averageness to shape her life. She could have told herself that she was not worthy of pushing for a more Islamic club. She could just as well use the excuse that her lack of intensive Islamic study (the kind that will qualify her to be an ustadha) was an impediment to doing *da'wah*. But no, Latifah rose to the challenge, put in the hard work, and undertook the risks (it's not easy to change a long-entrenched culture) necessary to make a difference to the world. *Alhamdulillah!*

So what does Latifah's story mean for you and me? Firstly, it means that each and every one of us has the capacity to make a difference to the world. We were not born to drag ourselves to work and then drag ourselves home to bed each day, *ad nauseum*. We were born as khalifahs (the stewards of this earth). We can, and we will, make a difference. We all have the potential within us. Second, making a difference doesn't mean having to achieve something of great grandeur, with great fanfare or million-dollar launches. Making a difference might mean, as in Latifah's case, pushing for your club (or family) to be more Islamic, or it might simply mean writing a letter every week to motivate others. A difference, no matter how small, is still a difference. And you never know how that difference might snowball into something beyond your wildest dreams!

Third, making a difference requires hard work, the determination to face challenges, and the courage to take risks. The Prophet Muhammad *sallallahu 'alayhi wa sallam* did not sit on a high throne and get people to feed him grapes. He went on the ground, he did what was required of him and more, and he was constantly serving the community and engaging in good actions. Making a difference requires you to live your life differently. And that's why ordinary people choose to only dream.

May Allah subhanahu wa ta'ala give us the strength to break our chains from the captivity of negative thought and to struggle in His path. Amin!

29

Journey to Allah, Path to Peace

Bismillah ir-Rahman ir-Rahim

I left my room, taking nothing but a notebook, a pen, and my keys. It was the first time in years that I had voluntarily decided to be without my gadgets; no iPad, no iPhone, no way to find me on the grid. After a long hectic week, my mind was exhausted. I had been so preoccupied with work and worries, that when I woke up the previous morning, the first thought in my mind was not one of gratitude, but of an inbox filled with emails and to-dos waiting for my action. That morning, I knew I was about to reach breaking point, and I just had to get away from it all before it was too late. And so I did.

I walked down the stairs, thinking of a nice spot to sit and write. The sun had been blanketed with clouds since morning, and there was a constant breeze that swirled in the air. The sky was a mix of blue and grey—as if wanting to give the best of both worlds—the scene of a beautiful day, coupled with the coolness of shade. I suddenly remembered the hockey field behind my hostel, and the rows of benches lining next to it. That was somewhere I could sit and think undisturbed, I made up my mind to go there.

Nearing the gates of the hostel, I could see the empty field ahead of me and was delighted that I would have it all to myself. But as I took another step, I realized that I could go no further. Bolted and chained, the gates were locked; it's no wonder the field was empty. I could feel my frustration starting to boil. But before I allowed it to fester in me like it did the entire week, I took a deep breath and told myself to let it go ... I desperately needed to let it go. Closing my eyes, I imagined bubbles of frustration drift out of me as I exhaled. I looked around. Behind me was a path that I had not walked for years. I decided to take it.

It is hard trying to silence a mind that has been full of anxiety for the longest time. While strolling along the path, I had to continuously resist the thoughts about work that crept into my subconscious. One second, I was peering into a forested area following the darting movements of a squirrel, and in the next I found myself thinking how I could improve the website I was building for a client. Again and again I found myself swatting thoughts away, ducking and swerving, determined to find the silence that I so needed and craved.

Slowly, the thoughts tired themselves out and the attacks became less frequent ... softer. I could hear my surroundings more clearly— the chorus of the birds as they flew in and out of trees, the bubbling of water gushing in the drain, the sharp crackle of leaves that danced in the wind—and I began to realize that the less I spoke to myself, the more I could hear the creations of Allah subhanahu wa ta'ala speak to me ... and thus, the more I could hear Him speak to me. The voice, His voice, was still not distinct, but I knew it was there, somewhere, and it was my task to find it once again.

At the end of the path, the trail forked into two. On my right was a path I travelled weekly on my way to campus—it was surrounded by buildings and shops, and lined with tired windows and the smell of fresh laundry. On my left was a path I had never taken. It was surrounded by gigantic trees, its floor covered with moss, fallen leaves and branches and other assorted gifts of nature, and most importantly, I had no idea where it would lead me. I stood rooted to the ground, easing my mind into silence. Suddenly, my left foot moved forward, as if it was pushed, and twigs crunched under the weight of my right; the path on the left had chosen me. And so did all the paths that manifested themselves after it.

Fifteen minutes later, I found myself atop a hill whose base I walked around every single morning. Since my first year on campus, I had always passed by that very same hill, often wondering what it must be like to sit on its peak and watch the greens and blues of the mountains beyond and the rolling clouds above. Finally, sitting barefoot on its green summit, I could at last report that the view was far better than I had imagined. I sat there, on the hill, for the longest time, not thinking nor saying anything but Allah's name. In the wide open sky I raised my hopes and dreams, and on the ground below I threw my anxieties and fears. Despite not saying or thinking anything, I knew that He knows all that there is to know.

In that brief moment I was just a lonely speck on the hill. He sent a cat to accompany me, which purred and brushed its beautiful white fur against my legs. The cat sat down next to me, and together we watched the birds dance in formation in the sky. For the rest of the hour-long walk I kept silent, and I asked everything else to speak to me.

***

Hearing the echo of students singing the chorus of a song, I stepped into the hostel from which the sounds were emanating. There I found walls covered with baby pink fabric and blue ribbons, and an assortment of colourful lollipops and sweets. I walked around the entire hostel, tracing the fabric and sweet wrappings with my fingers, enjoying the voices of the choir hovering in the air. Seeing a lone chair at the edge of an unkempt garden, I walked towards it, only to find myself surrounded by a swarm of playful brown and blue dragonflies. Further down, I was greeted by a view of the campus's river, and for several moments, found myself silently watching an old man fishing, casting the line with his fishing rod and reeling in a small fish.

Sitting on that bench in the middle of nowhere, I allowed myself to close my eyes and remain still, just focusing on the air that entered my lungs and the rush of air as I exhaled. Opening my eyes, I found a butterfly sitting atop my fingers, its wings brown with specks of yellow, its feelers sweeping against my skin. In that moment, I felt a calmness wash over me, the kind I have not experienced for an extremely long time. I smiled, my heart bursting with happiness, contentment and gratitude towards Him. I knew He had led me back to His presence, and had allowed me to hear His voice. He reminded me that I did not have to escape to a faraway beach or a remote village to find peace … peace is here, in my heart, in the remembrance of Him.

It was getting late. I could feel the breeze become more forceful, the sky getting darker. I threaded my way back along the path, letting my eyes wander and trying my best to see the different signs He was showing me. From between the trees I saw the hockey field and the benches I had wanted to sit on at the start of the walk. And then, it hit me. If I had focused my attention entirely on getting to where I wanted to go, and do everything and anything within my means to just get there as fast as I could, I would have missed the wonderful, silent, and breath-taking views and experiences that the journey had to offer.

I realized then that I needed to slow down my life. I needed to take on fewer roles and responsibilities, even though I know I could do them all. I needed to have the courage to let life surprise me, instead of trying too hard to control it in order to get to what I thought life had to offer. Message received, ya Robb. Message received.

It's nice to be with You and hear Your voice again. *Alhamdulillah*. May we never be too busy to listen, amin.

30

Feeling Lost at Sea?

Bismillah ir-Rahman ir-Rahim

I stared intently at the mountains on the horizon, wondering if my eyes were playing tricks on me. It was probably twenty minutes earlier that I had unceremoniously fallen asleep against the ferry's grimy windows, and I was pretty sure that the mountains I was now gazing at were the same ones that were there before I closed my eyes. I concluded that the ferry had, in fact, stopped in the middle of the wide sea. Another five minutes passed and the ship indeed appeared to be stationary; now, I was getting anxious. The murmur of the other passengers was quickly turning into a constant buzz in my ears. I shifted in my seat, trying to avoid the two overzealous women next to me, who probably had PhDs in the art of taking selfies, so involved were they in documenting every moment of their experience. Within the last thirty seconds, I had seen them taking selfies from a multitude of angles using no less than three devices: a DSLR, an iPad, and an iPhone on a monopod that was regularly thrust in my face. The *dhikr* (remembrances) taught by my mentor the day before, meant to keep my short temper in check, were quickly becoming handy.

My seat jerked forward. 'Sorry!' The blonde-haired, blue-eyed man behind me raised his hands in apology. I forced a grim smile. Breathe in ... breathe out. I craned my neck to look at the other passengers on board. Somewhere in the ferry I could hear voices beginning to complain to the crew about the delay. Some were asleep, and others, like me, sat anxious and helpless. Probably a handful were oblivious to the situation (like the doctorates in selfies), too caught up in their own activities. My eyes rested on a boy several rows behind who was silently peering out of the window. Curious, I stood up and tried to see what he was looking at.

There, swimming in deep water near the stern of the ferry with diving tanks strapped to their backs, were five or so crew members. Their faces held worried yet determined looks, and as they dived under and re-emerged from the choppy waters, the rough waves slammed into their faces, forcing them to gulp down mouthfuls of salt water. Positioned at the back of the ferry were more crew members, who lowered tools and equipment to the divers using thick ropes. There was a sense of urgency in the whole situation; the ferry must have broken down and they had to be the ones to fix it ... and fast.

Minutes passed. The ferry's engines sputtered and died again. Another diver disappeared into the sea, equipment in hand. He resurfaced a minute later. The ferry's engine sputtered for several seconds—I held my breath—then it roared into life, a steady 'putter-putter-putter' that broke the silence. The crew members in the water broke into smiles and began to hoist themselves back onto the ship.

'Yay!' The boy hollered, clapping his hands together with glee. His mother looked quizzically at him, confused by the sudden outburst of emotion from her otherwise-still son. I settled back into my seat, my pounding heart slowly settling into its normal rhythm. One of the doctors of selfies turned to her partner and asked: 'You mean we were not moving all this time?'

As the ferry throttled forward at full speed, He placed a thought in my mind. All of us, both you and I, are on this journey called life, whether we realize it or not. At times in this journey, we find ourselves 'stuck', just like the ferry I was on. In these moments, it seems like no matter what we do or how much we strive, we will feel as if the doors of *rizq* and blessings are closed to us—no job offers for months on end, no sight of our 'other half' despite years of prayers, no progress in grades despite burning the midnight oil for weeks.

Some of us, like the passengers who complained to the crew members, react by complaining and questioning Him and His plans. Others, like those asleep, shrug off the situation and in doing so void themselves of the lessons and growth that was offered to them. Many, like the selfie-takers, might even miss the blessings of the trial by being too absorbed and distracted by the illusions of the Dunya. And if you were like me and the other anxious passengers, we spend countless sleepless nights worrying about things that are essentially beyond our control.

Yet, among us is a rare breed of people who stand patiently by, like the boy, watching and knowing that there are forces working 'behind the scenes'. These people know that they will become unstuck in due time—in His time—a time that would be best for them. They place their full reliance and *tawakkul* (trust) in the One who manages the entirety of creation, knowing that things will work out fine in the end. And because of their patience and trust, they are awarded the sweetness of gratitude and happiness, and growth in their iman and character.

May Allah subhanahu wa ta'ala grant us the patience to undergo His trials, and the wisdom to see beyond the limitations of our knowledge, amin!

31

Who or What is Defining Who You Are?

Bismillah ir-Rahman ir-Rahim

I grew up with the mentality of a victim. For a long time I was convinced that I became this way either because of certain people entering my life, or certain circumstances that I had to go through. When bullies in school mocked me with hurtful words, I took what they said as true and thought of myself as they described. If they said I was naive and nerdy, then it must be true. When I did badly in my A-levels and could not get into any university, then the conclusion I reached was that I was not intelligent enough to have a degree. Since I was rejected, then I must be more stupid than all of my friends. I spent countless hours mulling over my fate, angry and depressed because I felt that life had dealt me all the losing cards. Why was I born this way? What can I do since I'm fated to have a life like this? Why is life just so unfair?

A couple of months ago I had a chat with an online friend on the subject of marriage. As we went deeper into the conversation and things became more personal, she unleashed one of the most hurtful sentences said to me in a long while: 'Of course, it's hard for you to find a man who wants to be with you; you're not soft and gentle like other girls. You should be like us normal girls, only then will you find someone who will love you.' Five minutes later I was in bed, crying, miserable and angry that I was not born with the soft demeanour that women were expected to have. Now, the funny thing is that for the past few years I considered my character to be my strength. I've often seen friends being bullied for their softness and I had leveraged my strength to help them get out of their situations. But in just a split second, an off-the-cuff remark made by an online friend shook me to the core and reshaped the way I thought about myself. In a single sentence, I became a victim once again.

As I lay there crying in bed, feeling sorry for myself, a friend entered the room and sat next to me. In between muffled sobs and wet tissues I told her what had just happened, and how frustrated I was that I am not softer or gentler or more woman-like.

'What makes you think you are not soft or gentle or woman-like?' She asked.

'Because (so-and-so) said so,' I replied.

'Has she met you? Has she spent hours and hours with you? Has she reached the level of intimacy with you that your close friends have?'

'No ... but we've been speaking and she's seen the way I act through my videos and stuff. I need to change to be like all of you.'

'Fadhilah, she does not know you. She knows a side of you, yes, but not all of you. She has not seen the soft and gentle side of you that only your family and friends have seen. Why are you letting her define you?'

'What do you mean, I am letting her define me? I am who I am.'

'But your definition of who you are is based on others' definition of you; In this case it's (her) description of you. Because you have not taken the time and effort to define who you are and what you believe of yourself, everything else in your life—the people you meet and the situations you find yourself in—will always define you. Why are you allowing others to define you and determine the course of your life?'

The tears dried up pretty quick after the realization hit me. The truth is that a large number of us are unknowingly caught in the same trap I was in. In the past several weeks alone, I had spoken to women who are intelligent and big-hearted, but are constantly allowing the people and circumstances surrounding them to define them, instead of consciously making the effort to define themselves.

I spoke with Nadira, a PhD holder with three beautiful and intelligent children who felt that she was never doing enough because of all the things she sees her friends post on social media. I spoke with Hafizah, a young, talented writer with a brilliant mind who felt that she can never accomplish anything in life because she was raised in 'just a normal, average family'. I spoke with Sida, one of the kindest, gentlest souls I know, who often spirals into cycles of depression because people kept making rude remarks about her and how she looked. It is easy to just go through the motions, accepting anything and everything that everyone says about us. What is harder is to consciously define ourselves so that we are able to steer our ship as captain.

When we drift along, we are, in essence, choosing to become victims of the ocean. Wherever the wind blows and the current flows, that's where we find ourselves moving; back and forth, going in circles, aimless and directionless. When we pick up the oars and choose to be the captain of the ship—our ship—we train ourselves to listen to the wind and to feel the currents that Allah subhanahu wa ta'ala sends our way, and use these instead as aids to help us get to where we want to be. So today, at this moment, take some time to ask yourself this question: 'Who or what is defining me?'

May Allah subhanahu wa ta'ala give us the courage and strength to be the captain of our own ship, and may He give us the knowledge and wisdom to be able to see ourselves in such a way that we only see Him. Amin!

32

Become Moulded by Allah Subhanahu Wa Ta'ala

Bismillah ir-Rahman ir-Rahim

It has been two weeks since I settled in *Zawīya* (a Sufi retreat) Ebrahim, South Africa. Since I touched down two Tuesdays ago, there have been a lot of things that I have been trying to accustom myself to; like the fact that I could not travel freely from one location to another (it's dangerous for women to drive alone and there is no public transportation available for 'foreigners'), or that the nights are so freezing cold on the farm that I had to sleep with several layers of clothes and two thick blankets (and still managed to shiver underneath it all). The hardest thing for me, probably, is the fact that this is the first time I was this far away from my family and friends, and that it's really expensive to call home or to get online; it can get extremely lonely when you're in a foreign land with no one to share your experiences. I've always believed that I'm the kind of person who would find no problem leaving the nest, so feeling all the different (sad) emotions welling up in me really caught me off guard.

But I guess that's what's expected when you take yourself out of your comfort zone. You discover all sorts of ideas surfacing in your mind that you never thought you would have. You stumble upon emotions and feelings that you never knew you had in you. You find in yourself the beginnings of an intense struggle and the desire to flee. And not surprisingly, many people choose to flee. For the most part of my life, I know I did. When maths got too complex, I stopped attending classes; when my hockey coach drummed up our training exponentially, I pulled out; when *tajwid* lessons got too complicated, I zoned out. When the going got tough, I quit. I chose to flee.

What I didn't understand then is that the struggle is the 'rite of passage' for growth, the *fitrah* (natural disposition) that precedes Allah's gift of a better you. Mawlana Jalal ad-Din Muhammad Rumi, a thirteenth-century Persian Sufi, compares our whole lives to this process of kneading, shaping, and fashioning:

> My soul remembers its source:
> I was in the potter's hands while
> he mixed clay and water—
> a new home for me, I think.
> The kiln is hot. I'm trying to escape!
> Willing, unwilling—what does it matter?
> No longer resisting, I get kneaded and moulded,
> just like every other lump of clay.[6]

---

6. Neil Douglas-Klotz, *The Sufi Book of Life: 99 Pathways of the Heart for the Modern Dervish* (London, New York: Penguin Compass, 2005).

Allah subhanahu wa ta'ala posits countless opportunities for us to become better versions of ourselves. As Shaykh Ebrahim says, every moment is an unfolding of a story meant uniquely for us, and our ability to grow is determined by what we give to that moment.

So when a door of opportunity is opened for us and we choose to flee, we are essentially not giving to that moment what it requires of us. Hence, we deny ourselves of the opportunity to grow. When we resist the potter's hands and repel the hot kiln, we remain but a shapeless lump of clay our entire lives. This Ramadan, take some time to reflect how Allah subhanahu wa ta'ala is moulding you in various aspects of your life: from your spiritual journey to your relationships, from your beliefs to your character. Notice the struggle from within, and reframe your mind to think of it as an opportunity; as Allah subhanahu wa ta'ala's hands mould you with His infinite love and unmatched wisdom. Choose not to flee, choose not to resist, but to embrace the struggle as it knocks on your door. *'Truly, Allah does not change the conditions of the people unless they change themselves.'* (al-Ra'd 13:11)

In a few minutes, the imam of the *zawiya* will probably knock on my door with his *adhan* recitation for congregational Fajr prayers, just as he (or another brother from the *zawiya*) does for every obligatory prayer of the day. Honestly, I have never done so many consecutive congregational prayers in my entire life (nor as many *dhikr* or saying 'Alhamdulillah'), and if I had resisted or chosen to flee, I would have pretty much missed out on all the wonderful gifts Allah subhanahu wa ta'ala has in store for me for this Ramadan.

Alhamdulillah. May we allow ourselves to be moulded by His loving hands, amin!

33

Destined to be Muslim

Bismillah ir-Rahman ir-Rahim

'In retrospect,' she said, her blonde fringe sweeping over her eyes as she spoke, 'I guess I was destined to be a Muslim since I was born; I just did not know it yet.'

I was intrigued, 'What do you mean?' The question hung in the air inside the Toyota, lingering as the South African terrain rolled past us, a blur of never-ending orange floor and bright blue sky that went on as far as the eyes could see.

'As a journalist, I was always sent to Muslim countries, and I was often surrounded by Muslims and by extension, Islam. But I couldn't really see the beauty of it at that time; I was looking with the eyes of a sceptical Westerner, tainted with certain … presumptions.'

There was a pothole in the ground. Bump! Little Saadiah cried out on the back seat. The car rolled to a stop by the side of the road. 'What did you keep assuming?'

She laughed, crouching over trying to pick up the raisins that fell from her daughter's grasp. There was silence for a moment as she travelled back in time; I could almost hear the whirring of her mind. 'You know; that Islam was backwards, that Muslim women were not allowed to be educated, that Muslim women were oppressed: death by stoning and all that.' The car moved again, slowly picking up speed.

I flipped through articles and news broadcasts from the likes of CNN and Newsweek for the past several years in my mind—that description was just about right.

'So one day, right here in South Africa, my ex, who is an Emmy award-winning photographer, invited me to come along to a talk he was attending in order to shoot a documentary on Islam I didn't want to join him—backward Muslims and all that—but he kept on insisting that it was my cup of tea.' We paused for a moment as she looked for incoming traffic at the junction.

'So I went with him, and was really pleasantly surprised that I truly enjoyed the experience!'

'What about it did you like?'

'How open and welcoming they were to non-Muslims, how intellectually stimulating the discourse was, the wonderful and intelligent people

I met, but mostly,' she paused, perhaps reliving the moment in that split second, 'the love, warmth, and sense of community that I could feel in my heart; one that I didn't think I've felt anywhere else, ever.'

I smiled as I recalled my last few weeks with the people of *Zawiya Ebrahim*, and the warm and vibrant Muslims I've been introduced to along the way; the genuine hugs, smiling eyes, the sense of childish happiness and contentment that emanated from them as we drummed to the beats of the *dhikr* and *Salawat* (praises of the Prophet *sallallahu 'alayhi wa sallam*). I could see the colours that she painted.

'So I kept returning to the centre a couple of times, you know, just to be around these people.'

'And that's how you converted to Islam?'

'Well, yes, and no. I was still years away from my conversion; I stopped going to the centre for several years because, well, life happened, and the voice in my mind was still stronger than the one in my heart. But one day, a friend of mine who was searching for God showed me this pamphlet of a talk she wanted to go to, and it turned out that it was the exact same centre I used to attend! So I went with her, and I was again, for the lack of a better word, addicted.

'Somewhere between those talks, my friends and I went on a spiritual retreat, kind of like a meditation camp. I was having a raging flu and fever and was up to my neck in meds, numbing me of my usual train of thought, and maybe that, and the meditation, made me experience something totally out of this world.'

'What's that?' I asked, hungry for more. The car was practically moving at a snail's pace as the world seemed to stand still, waiting for her explanation.

'As I was meditating, still and silent, I could literally hear my heart saying, over and over again: *la ilaha illa Allah, la ilaha illa Allah, la ilaha illa Allah.*'

'*Subhan Allah.* That's beautiful!'

'Beautiful, but scary for me. I was brought up a Christian, but I've long stopped practising and had fully embraced the fact that my life was one without a path. To even have that feeling of wanting to submit to a god or to take on a religion was extremely daunting, and I still had remnants of the Western attitude towards Muslims and Islam.'

The Toyota's engines whirred to a stop as we found a parking lot. I turned to face her, the silence in the car more profound than ever.

'I went to the centre again the next day, my mind and heart in sorts. And the Imam, he said something which I felt was directed specially to me. He said, "Do not feel pressured to convert to Islam." *Subhan Allah*, the moment he acknowledged what I was feeling, I could feel all the pressure being released, and on that day, right after that talk, I went up to him and said my *shahadah*. I've never felt so relieved my entire life!'

I smiled. From the rays of the sun, I could make out the tears that glistened in her eyes.

'You remember I mentioned earlier that I felt like I was meant to be a Muslim since I was born?'

I nodded my head.

'I am Dutch, and by right, my parents were supposed to give me a Dutch name. But my Mum couldn't be bothered as she felt it was too long, and so she took the acronyms of what was supposed to be my name, and made that my name instead.

'When the Imam asked for my name upon my giving the *shahadah*, he laughed, and said that I already had a name common in the Muslim world!'

We both laughed as little Saadiah giggled on the back seat, as if understanding the conversation all along. I pried the door open, the South African winter greeting me as soon as I stepped out of the car.

'He gave me the best advice I could receive as a fresh convert too, that Imam.'

'What's that?'

'That firstly, if I wanted to learn Islam, don't look at the Muslims.'

I cracked up till my sides hurt.

'And secondly, that whatever happens in my journey, I need to remember to love Allah more than I love Islam, to love Allah more than any ustadh or shaykh, to love Allah more than any Sufi (or Salafi) thought that I might subscribe to.'

We were silent for a moment, each deep in thought. It felt surreal to me that we were having this conversation; a Dutch convert from the countryside of South Africa and a Malay-Muslim from an island-city located on the other side of the world, crossing paths at the exact moment when I needed to learn a lesson and to love a person. I was deeply humbled: 'Thank you, Esma for sharing your story with me.'

Esma threw a smile my way as we walked side-by-side, little Saadiah linking us together with her tiny little hands. Even though we've had and will have differences in opinion, I was determined to make that love I felt for Esma a relationship that is born out of love for a fellow human being that Allah subhanahu wa ta'ala has created and guided.

Ella Susanna Maria Anderson: Esma.

May we always be open to chance encounters, may we always be full of love and warmth for others, and may we always be able to see beauty in others, amin.

34

Of Veiling and Unveiling and Seeing the Wisdom of Everything

Bismillah ir-Rahman ir-Rahim

I am a firm believer that when you sincerely ask Allah subhanahu wa ta'ala for guidance, He will respond to you. While I know people who lament that Allah subhanahu wa ta'ala does not answer in times of trials because He is testing us (like a teacher would be quiet in an examination), I truly, honestly, believe that is not the case. I believe that it is our veils that prevent us from receiving that guidance and light from Him.

I remember once reading a story about a Sufi who praised Allah subhanahu wa ta'ala for everything, in every situation. When he received some good news, he said *Alhamdulillah*. When he received some bad news, he too said *Alhamdulillah*. In short, he said *Alhamdulillah* for every single thing that happened in his life. I did not really think much about the story at that time, but as I continued walking on the Path, it struck me why the Sufi was able to say that. Because he did not have any veils covering him, he had nothing to prevent him from seeing the beauty in the narrative Allah subhanahu wa ta'ala had written for him. Thus, there is no 'bad' incident per se, to the Sufi every single moment is the unravelling of a complete, beautiful story that Allah subhanahu wa ta'ala has written for him, one that is meant to incite a sense of heightened consciousness, awe, amazement and, yes ... gratitude. *Alhamdulillah!*

The second thing that struck me was the concept of veiling itself. I often ask myself why some people could easily see the wisdom and beauty in a given situation, while others (okay, me) could only see the wisdom a long ... long ... long ... time after the situation has taken place. For instance, in 2006, I did terribly in my GCSE A-levels and couldn't get into any of the local universities in Singapore. It was a pretty sore point for me because I'd prayed hard to do well, and when I saw the Cs, Ds, and Es on my result slip, I felt that God had abandoned me. And so I did what any silly immature person would do ... I abandoned God.

I felt angry and cheated, and so for the next few years I refused to have anything to do with Him. I ran as far in the opposite direction as I could. It was only in 2010, four years later, when I was accepted into an Islamic University, that I finally understood why I failed my A-levels ... it was so that I would end up in that particular Islamic University where my life would eventually turn 180 degrees! *Alhamdulillah!* The thing is, when I reflect back on those four years, it dawned on me that He had been sending me guidance all the while, but it was I who had veiled myself from receiving them by giving attention to my negative thoughts instead.

For example, a week or so after my terrible results came out, my mother had actually suggested that I apply to the very same Islamic University ... but I scoffed at her. I had numerous invitations from family and friends alike to attend religious classes, but I turned my nose up at them. Throughout the four years, I was able to gain work experience in both private and public sectors, earn a pretty decent pay (for someone without a diploma/degree), get a certificate in Multimedia Design ... but still I felt that God wasn't there for me. Why? It was all because I was too caught up in my own narrative— the selfish, anxious thoughts of self-victimization in my head—that I was veiled from seeing and understanding His narrative! In essence, I realized that I am my own barrier to God. I am the one that chose not to see Him. I am my own veil! *Subhan Allah* ...

At the *zawiya* I currently live in, the people of the Path like to conclude our *dhikr* and *wird* sessions with this du'a': 'O Allah, grant us annihilation in You. Grant us death before we die.' For a long time I never quite understood that du'a', and would hesitate from saying Amin. But one day I finally plucked up the courage to ask the Imam of the *zawiya*, who explained (I'm summarizing) that death is what will finally stop Man from all of his wants in this Dunya, and death is the point where the believer has nothing else to chase, nowhere else to go, except to return to his Rabb. So the meaning of the concept of 'annihilation in You' and 'death before we die' is to be able to live a life where nothing truly matters and nothing is left for a person except Allah. In essence, it means to remove all the veils that make the 'I', so that all that's left is 'Him'!

We say 'la ilaha illa Allah', there is no God but Allah, but the truth is many among us unknowingly make ourselves and our *nafs*, our god.

And in doing so, we veil ourselves from Him, voluntarily withdrawing ourselves from His Mercy. And in that, He—as He has mentioned in the Qur'an—makes us 'deaf, dumb, and blind—so they will not return [to the right path]'. (al-Baqarah 2: 18) After all that's said in this letter, I must acknowledge that to remove the 'I' from the self is perhaps the hardest thing to ever achieve in this life. It's an ongoing process, an ongoing struggle, the bigger jihad that resides within each and every one of us.

However, just because It's hard and seemingly impossible does not mean that we don't try. And we try by taking small steps towards Him, away from our selves. We try by telling ourselves to look for the wisdom in every situation. We try by telling ourselves 'Alhamdulillah'. Alhamdulillah for all things, big and small. Alhamdulillah.

May our tongue, limbs and heart always be beating to the rhythm of Alhamdulillah! Amin!

35

Overcoming the Worries of Tomorrow

Bismillah ir-Rahman ir-Rahim

So much has happened since my last letter. I've celebrated my twenty-sixth birthday, concluded my time interning for Shaykh Ebrahim at Schuitema Human Excellence, went on my first solo adventure in Cape Town, and finally returned home to Singapore to be in the company of family and friends, whom I have yet to spend genuine time with since I began my study in the International Islamic University of Malaysia four years ago. Oh! And did I tell you I graduated sometime in the past month as well? No? Well, I've finally completed my degree in Human Sciences (Communications) with a minor in Islamic Knowledge. *Alhamdulillah!*

This morning as I write to you, I am filled with humbleness and gratefulness to Allah subhanahu wa ta'ala. To tell you the truth, I haven't felt that way since I returned. The moment I set foot in the country over a week ago, I've been bombarded with questions and opinions from all corners:

- What are you going to do now? (Answer: Still thinking).

- When are you getting married? (Answer: Still looking).

- Have you gotten a job? (Answer: Still deciding if I should consider the offers).

- You should do your Masters since it will be paid for. (Answer: Mum doesn't look too happy with me flying off again.)

- You should work and repay your parents. (Answer: So ... I can't continue my studies?)

- You should get married and save your *din*. (Answer: Where can I buy a husband?)

- Why have you gained weight? (Answer: ... .) Etc., etc.

The result of being on the receiving end of the questions and opinions have led me to feeling rather nervous and anxious this past week or so. My mind was constantly whirring with lists of pros and cons, and my heart was constantly heavy, fearful of making a decision that would most definitely disappoint someone ... my parents, or my lecturers, or maybe even myself. At the other end, my bank account was increasingly getting lighter. I was a worrying wreck!

Yesterday, however, I forced myself to tear away from the world of worries, and reopened one of my favourite books, *The Millennium Discourses*. On the very first page, Shaykh Ebrahim writes:

> Peace is not full of something. The more full you are of things, the more disturbed your being is. The noisier your inner dialogue is, the more you ramble on inside your mind about your concerns, your fears, and your hopes, the less peace you have. It is precisely the fact that we are always talking to ourselves about what we would like to have and what we wish to avoid, that we are in a state of agitation, in a place where we have no peace or fulfilment.

So much truth in that paragraph, *subhan Allah*; the ramblings had even become a veil for me in my prayers!

Realizing that I'd lost the plot again, I disconnected from the world and in an attempt to silence my inner dialogue, decided to do something to my room, which had not been touched since I left for Malaysia four years earlier. As I began clearing and unpacking my things, I stumbled upon pictures of my farewell parties and letters from family and friends, making du'a' for my hijrah. I read notes of encouragement when I was struggling with school, and I read messages of congratulations when Allah subhanahu wa ta'ala made my journey easy and fruitful. It didn't take long for gratitude and immense relief to wash over me.

If Allah subhanahu wa ta'ala had taken care of everything perfectly for me for the past four years (or rather, the past twenty-six), why am I using up all my energy worrying about what is in store for me in the present and in the future? What is ungratefulness and stupidity but thinking that it is I who determine my success or failure? Allah! What a reminder! *Alhamdulillah!*

When we look into the future, a lot of us see an unknown, we see uncertainty, and it drives us crazy because we feel as if we need to set in place the elements that give us some control over it. The truth of the matter is that whatever perceived control we feel we have put in place is nothing but an illusion. We can spend all our time worrying, planning and plotting for our five-year plans, but may face death in the next five minutes. The reality is that this moment, right now, is all that we have. We can choose to spend it worrying about an illusory tomorrow, or we can choose to spend it by acting consistently with the courtesy of the situation, by giving the moment we are facing the attention that it is due.

As Shaykh Ebrahim says in the *The Millennium Discourses*:

> When you pay what Allah asks of you in the moment, then by His Rahmat, He will give you many multiples more than you could ever have imagined. This is the extraordinary nature of His design … In other words, when you deal with the situation in front of you on the basis of what Allah [subhanahu wa ta'ala] wants from you, what you should be contributing, you are increased and you grow. You change beyond measure. Whereas, if you confront the situation on the basis of your desires, when you want to get out of the situation, then you are frozen there.

You are delayed at the gate.

May Allah subhanahu wa ta'ala grant us annihilation in Him. May He grant us death before we die. Amin.

36
❧

The Wisdom of the Elderly

Bismillah ir-Rahman ir-Rahim

Eid Mubarak *wa taqabalallahu minna wa minkum* everybody!

I hope all of you had a good time with family and friends this Eid, *Alhamdulillah*. My family and I went to see one of my favourite uncles yesterday, a humble man nearing seventy years old—still active at the *masjid*—and who, in his life, had started and sold numerous businesses, one of which operates worldwide.

The Prophet Muhammad *sallallahu 'alayhi wa sallam* said in a hadith, 'O Muslims! Sit with your elders, ask the scholars, and meet wise people.' In today's letter I'd like to share with you four of the many nuggets of wisdom my uncle shared with my siblings and I yesterday. May they benefit, *insha' Allah*!

Wisdom 1: You will get what you intend for (Bidhnillah)

In the course of his international business travels, my uncle had the opportunity to meet people from all around the world. In light of the Hajj celebrations, my uncle shared that one of the most inspiring people he had ever met was an Indonesian who managed to save up enough money for the pilgrimage even though all that he knew to do was to fish and sell his catch at the market. He did this, day in and day out, for years.

'How did you manage to save up this much?' My uncle asked.

'Because when I first started work, the first intention I ever made was that my work will bring me enough *rizq* to go to Hajj.'

Relating the story to us, my uncle laughed and shook his head. 'It's that easy; you get what you intend for. I've met many other Muslims around the world whose intentions when they get a job are to buy a new car, a new home, pay for their children's education, etc. But Indonesia is the only country so far I've been to where I've met numerous youths whose intentions when they get their first job is to go to Hajj. And so ... they get what they intend for, and we get what we intend for.'

Wisdom 2: Speak well or be silent

'The human heart is flesh and blood; it is not made of wood and stones,' my uncle mused. He had just shared with us a story about how one of his contacts had maligned him.

'There is a Malay proverb which says that a person can paddle his canoe back when he has gone too far downstream, but words cannot be recalled once spoken,' said my uncle, 'so learn to not speak ill of others or even to speak badly to others, for the heart is soft and easily hurt.'

I remember listening to a lecture by Shaykh Ebrahim saying that we should always be very careful of what we say, because sometimes something that might be trifle to us, when spoken, might sit in the heart of someone subconsciously and grow to become a negative echo within them:

> The first rule of speaking has to be to bear in mind what you are saying in the consciousness of somebody else, because very often what we say to another person is very viral in character. It's an apparently small idea, but the touch of unkindness often festers in the other person. You do not put this virus in the other person and you walk away, and this virus eats up the person for days and months afterwards.

Wisdom 3: Smile

'How did you manage to build such a wide network of friends and contacts, uncle?' I asked. Often when I went out with him, people from all walks of life would come up to him just to say hi.

'Speak only when needed, but smile to everyone all the time.' He smiled.

Wisdom 4: Always be learning

As we were having our lunch, my uncle started asking me about my plans for the future. When I told him of my current freelance work developing websites and helping businesses navigate their way online, his eyes lit up and with the excitement of a child, he started asking me questions about ecommerce and online marketing.

Now, this is a man who is already sixty-eight years old, and who, by the end of this year, would step down from his position in an international company. Also, bear in mind that this is a man who has built, from the ground up, many businesses and employed numerous workers. And yet, the very same man was choosing to continue to educate himself despite his age, and even learning from a younger person!

I've been reading a lot about having a 'fixed mind-set' vs a 'growth mind-set', and I think my uncle is a perfect example of a person holding a growth mind-set: he is always seeking to learn new things and better himself despite the odds. I think it's this attitude of always learning, in both aspects of the Dunya and the Akhirah, that all of us need to embed in us if we were to aspire success, *bidnihillah*.

May we learn to always learn from others, from the elders, the scholars, and the wise. Amin!

37

Are You Making Smart Investments?

'As humans, we invest in many areas of our life. We invest in our physical form, perhaps through keeping our body healthy or in securing our finances. We invest in our intellectual aspect, by going to school and getting a degree, or perhaps even taking up more skills. And a lot of us, without realizing it, invest in our emotional aspect, through activities that expand our social circle and enrich our social life,' explained the ustadh. He was pacing about the room excitedly, drawing charts on the whiteboard to explain the purpose of his company.

'But,' he paused, looking at me squarely in the eye, 'while most of us spend a lot of time investing in these three aspects, we often forget to invest in the most crucial area of our life—the one that lasts long after our body crumbles to dust—our Spirit.'

I found myself nodding, and for a split second, was reminded of two different stories shared with me by fellow readers of these letters:

Story 1, as told by a journalist

The food stall was buzzing with lunchtime activity; it was hard to make conversation but the topic at hand was interesting. 'Did lots of Singapore Muslims get to go for Hajj this year?' asked Dalina, as the four of us dug into our meals. I've known Dalina for over a year now. We've exchanged emails a dozen times or so and bumped into each other in lectures, but this was the first proper lunch date. She is a journalist by profession, and I kind of expected the question to come sooner or later as the Hajj season had just passed.

'Well, the Saudi government has a quota on the number of people who can go, and from what we've heard, the number of visas granted has been decreasing,' a friend answered. 'The waiting list can reach years!'

'It's the same here in my country,' Dalina noted, 'and the sad thing is, I know many rich and elite people who make the trip to Makkah countless times each year. Makes me wonder how many of the poor are not able to go because the visas have been taken up by people who have already made the trip.' She paused, as if to decide whether she should continue speaking.

'I cover these people regularly. Let's just say that some of them, upon returning each time, are even worse off than they were before they left. Going to Makkah is like a holiday for them!' Dalina elaborated, a crease making its mark on her forehead: 'Sometimes I wish some of them can invest their money better by sending poor pious Muslims to Umrah or Hajj instead.'

Story 2, as shared by a reader via email
'I read your last letter about your uncle and I totally agree with you and the Hadith about sitting with the elderly, scholars and wise people. I've been living with my grandparents for as long as I can remember and the things they have taught me directly and indirectly have made a deep impact on the way I look at things.

'Just to give you an example, my grandmother would regularly search for advertisements in the newspaper for things on which she can make *waqf* (an inalienable charitable endowment under Islamic law). Each time I accompanied her to do the *waqf* transaction, it struck me that not only did she make *waqf* under her own name, but also on behalf of all those who have passed: her parents, her parents-in-law whom she has never even met, her husband, son, and even her uncle, who taught her the basics of 'alif-ba-ta' (the Arabic alphabet). She also makes *waqf* on behalf of the living—my family, my uncles and aunts, and my cousins as well. Of course she tries to make it as discreet as possible, but she needs my help to write their names on the form. And I see my name each time, *Alhamdulillah*.

'One day, curiosity got the better of me and I asked her why she does what she does. She replied—and I paraphrase—"On the Day when I cannot even help myself from the punishment of Allah subhanahu wa ta'ala, this is the least I can do to try and help my family. I don't want to enjoy the rewards of Allah subhanahu wa ta'ala alone, I want to share it with all of you, no matter how small it is, because there is no such thing as a small deed in the eyes of Allah subhanahu wa ta'ala if the deed was done in sincerity."

'That, sis Fadhilah, to me is true love.'

So, are we making smart investments?
In the first story, we see a group of people who are making an investment in their Spiritual aspect through repeated trips to Hajj and Umrah. In the second, we see an old lady making an investment in not just her own Spiritual aspect, but also that of her loved ones, by making *awqaf* under all their names.

I'd like to be clear that I am not comparing one against the other, nor am I saying that one triumphs the other (*wallahua'lam*). However, as the ustadh reminded me, we are all constantly making investments in our life through the decisions we take—and perhaps it is high time that we look critically at our investments and their returns. If we have been given the *rizq* of abundant wealth, what investments are we making with them? Are we investing to further increase our physical gains, or to better our education, or to gain His blessings? If we have been given the *rizq* of a certain skill or an intellectual mind, what investments are we making with them? Are we using them for our own profit in this world, or are we using them to benefit the whole of mankind and to spread His message?

Investments require capital and resources; ones you may have today, but not tomorrow. As the Prophet *sallallahu 'alayhi wa sallam* said: 'Take benefit of five before five: Your youth before your old age, your health before your sickness, your wealth before your poverty, your free time before you are preoccupied, and your life before your death.' (Hadith, narrated by Ibn 'Abbas and reported by al-Hakim)

May we be given the *rizq* to invest our youth, health, wealth, free time, and life itself in His way. Amin!

38

A Practical Guide to Saving the World

Bismillah ir-Rahman ir-Rahim

My heart became heavier the longer I poured over the paper. My inner dialogue was filled with disbelief: 'How can it be? This is not possible! Isn't Islam on the rise?' But the studies spoke for themselves … The number of Muslim divorce cases are getting higher, the disintegration of Muslim family structures are an increasing phenomenon, and family genealogies are becoming increasingly complex. The bubble I had lived in while I was away studying for four years popped; welcome home. Welcome to reality, Fadhilah. This is the real world you're living in.

A Tale of a Boy

'Ten years ago, the cases of troubled juveniles were straightforward,' said the researcher. 'They were usually the offspring of divorced parents, or parents who were too busy working to give their children the attention they need. But now ...' his voice trailed off. His shoulders slumped and his face was troubled.

'But now?' I probed.

'Let me share with you the story of a boy I met recently in my line of work. He's thirteen, his parents are married but are not together in the traditional sense. His father is having an affair with a married woman, whose husband is also having an affair with another married woman. His mother is having an affair with another man, whose wife is also seeing someone else. They are all aware of each other's activities, and yet no one cares. In fact, this boy sees, in his home, different women and men waltzing in and out all the time. He sits in his corner, and he sees his mum with a different man. And the next day he sees his dad coming in with a new woman in his arms.'

My jaw was on the floor.

'And these irresponsible parents only get worse. All of them—from his own parents to the men and women they are having affairs with—are addicted to drugs and are thus unable to care for themselves properly, let alone their children. This boy I met? The reason he's in my files is because the police caught him stealing food at the market ... for his father.'

'*Astaghfirullāh*,' my heart was growing heavier by the minute. 'And this is a Muslim family?'

'Yes. And this boy's story is not an isolated case! My cabinet is filled with stories like his. Is it no wonder then that he ends up so defeated and terrified, until he finally learns to mask his brokenness by acting out against the world?'

A heavy silence hung in the air around us. My thoughts wandered. How true it is that Allah subhanahu wa ta'ala created opposites in order for us to be truly grateful and appreciative of what we experience. How can we feel joy if we don't feel pain? How can we feel peace if we have not experienced discontent? How can we truly appreciate the simple blessings of a complete family, when we don't see the trials that other families are made to go through?

'How do we reverse this? How do we help boys like him? How do we help change society for the better?'

'You don't have to change society. You just have to change you, and then your families.'

Shaykh Hamza Yusuf and Imam Zaid Shakir said in their book *Agenda to Change our Condition* that 'the family is the first and most important unit of society and is designed to nurture and prepare the young to carry on the civilizational enterprise.'[7] In essence, the world is made up of communities, communities are made up of societies, and

---

7.   Hamza Yusuf and Zaid Shakir, *Agenda to Change our Condition* (Berkeley, CA: Sandala, 2013).

societies are made up of families—the smallest group structure. After families, the group then gives way to the individual: You.

What this means is how you act and carry yourself will have an effect on your family. And how your family acts will, no matter how small, affect the society, and so on and so forth. Multiply families millions of times and you get the population of the world.

> 'O you who have believed, protect yourselves and your families from a Fire whose fuel is people and stones, over which are (appointed) angels, harsh and severe; they do not disobey Allah in what He commands them but do what they are commanded.' (al-Tahrim 66: 6)

It is simple in theory: if you as a parent (or a future parent) show your children nothing but love and affection, and raise them in an environment where they learn to give to others for the sake of Allah subhanahu wa ta'ala, then *insha' Allah* these children will grow up with a world-view similar to yours. Likewise, if you carry yourself selfishly and walk the earth with vanity and disdain, then your family—your children—will most likely carry the same world-view that you hold, even as they enter into adulthood. After all, as Shaykh Ebrahim explains, to understand a concept we first have to look at the first manifestation of that concept ... and first manifestations of concepts are usually in the parent–child relationship. Change the world by changing you.

We often view change as a strong force, an awakening of whole societies working together for the greater good. We think of it as a tide that rushes in, crushing everything old and broken and starting with a clean slate. From where we stand we sign petitions, we wire our contributions, we scream with our fingers on our laptops and mobile phones: 'We want change!' But what if ... what if change is also in the subtleties? What if change is the soft wind that shapes the desert and the cliffs over centuries? What if change is also the soft whisper in our hearts that remind us to be better, to improve; to return to Him? What if change begins with the small hand that wraps itself around our finger, eyes hopeful, waiting to be painted with the different colours of our soul? What if saving the world begins with your families? What if saving the world begins with you?

May Allah subhanahu wa ta'ala plant the seeds of change within us and allow us to bear its fruits to the *ummah*. Amin!

39

Your Journey Hints at Your End

Bismillah ir-Rahman ir-Rahim

I looked out of the window at the streams of children passing through the school gates. The clothes on their back were uniform, a pale yellow top and green skirt, carefully pressed, but the expressions they wore were anything but the same. Just minutes earlier, teachers had handed over slips of paper that determined the academic trajectory of nervous twelve year-olds around the nation. It was easy to guess which path a child was to embark on by their expression ... or more so of their parents who were there to meet them.

For a moment, I caught sight of a small, dark-skinned child sprinting across the road. Her short bangs splayed across her forehead as she pushed against the wind. In her hands, she grasped the same paper the others carried. Unlike them though, she was alone. No fussing mother or doting father; just her, and that piece of paper. I lost sight of her for a second as she disappeared into the building. Then I heard her steps coming up the stairwell, quick and heavy as she used each step as a launch pad to the next. For a moment there was silence, then her small body crashed through the door of my apartment.

'Mum! I got top of the class!' The child blurted out, barely able to contain her news any longer. I glanced at the door. My 12-year-old self grinned back.

Just as she pushed herself into the forefront of my memories, she vanished. In her place stood an 18-year-old. The child's wide smile and laughing eyes were gone; in this young woman nothing but sorrow remained. In her hands she held a similar paper to the one grasped so excitedly six years earlier, but the contents were starkly different. What used to be As were now Ds, and what used to be a bright future is now bleak. A tear ran down her cheek, then another, then another, before they all tumbled out one after another, unstoppable.

A car honked down the street, snapping me back to the present. And yet I found my heart still heavy, chained to the past. One examination, two possible ends: the child running home, bursting with happiness and contentment at a bright future; the teenager dragging her feet, crushed and disheartened, a black abyss waiting ahead. Which will I feel again when I receive the results of the most important examination, the only one that matters, on the Day of Judgment?

The more I reflected on the matter, the sharper my focus became on the ghosts of my past. My 12-year-old self: innocent and naive, head buried in books, hand in my mother's. If I was not reading or playing the games that children play, I was made to sit with the elders to recite the Qur'an or listen to a lecture. My 18-year-old self: bored and brash, always finding my way out of responsibilities. If I was not sneaking out of my home or escaping from school, I was concocting the next lie to get into things I was not supposed to. Is it not fitting that each of my pasts finally faced an end best suited to their actions? You are your end.

We often make du'a' for Allah subhanahu wa ta'ala to grant us a *husnul khatimah* (good end), and to protect us from a *sul khatimah* (bad end). But as we make the intention on our lips and in our hearts, we have to remember that intention alone does not cut it; attention too plays a part in getting our intentions to where they aspire to be. What are we paying attention to as we traverse from one day to the next? What are we spending our time on this week? Who are we seated with for the most of today? What have we been talking about the past hour? Who is occupying our thoughts right at this very moment? Is it Allah subhanahu wa ta'ala?

While we make du'a' for the mercy of Allah subhanahu wa ta'ala and the blessed intervention of our Prophet Muhammad *sallallahu 'alayhi wa sallam* on the Day of Judgment, we too have to strive to be vigilant about what we dedicate our attention to while we are in this Dunya. The Prophet Muhammad *sallallahu 'alayhi wa sallam* said that we will be with whom we love. If today, we find ourselves engaged and giving all our attention to the Dunya, then we can expect the Dunya to be with us in the Akhirah. But if we find ourselves immersed in the remembrance of Allah subhanahu wa ta'ala and our actions are for His sake, then we can, *insha' Allah*, expect our remembrance and deeds to be resurrected as testimonies for us in the Akhirah. Our end will be, *bidhnillah*, a mirror of our thoughts and actions, a reflection of our intentions and attention.

As my attention drifted back to the children leaving the schoolyard, it struck me that there is one huge difference between the results they just received, and the results that all of us will be given one day: the former is temporary, and the latter ... eternal. Allah.

May Allah subhanahu wa ta'ala place His light in our hearts and keep us on His path. May He forgive our sins—known and unknown—and give us the blessings of His Rahmah. May He gift us the best of intentions and the most beautiful of attention. May He make us the child that runs home to Him, happy and content. Amin.

40

The Prophet's Touch

Bismillah ir-Rahman ir-Rahim

It was the Prophet's *sallallahu 'alayhi wa sallam* return to Makkah after years of being in exile. He had left his home—the resting place of his beloved wife Sayyidatina Khadījah *radhiallahu 'anha*—with just the company of Sayyidina Abu Bakr as-Siddique *radhiallahu 'anhu*. But this time, as he stood at the gates of Makkah once again, behind him were his companions; an estimated 30,000 in all. He could have marched in with the pompousness of a conqueror, standing tall in front of his army and crushing the hearts of the Quraysh with fear. He had every reason to do so; for years they had called him a madman and mocked his message, tortured and starved those who responded to his call, and forced him out of the very land filled with memories of those he had loved and lost.

And yet ... the Prophet *sallallahu 'alayhi wa sallam* divided the companions, and asked that they enter Makkah through different routes so as not to scare the Quraysh with their numbers. Reminding them not to shed blood unless attacked, he then rode into Makkah, head bowed, on the back of his mule, with nary a hint of self-pride nor thought of vengeance and retaliation. Despite this, the people of Makkah ran with fear in all directions. How could they expect safe passage from the man upon whose life they had inflicted such misery and hardship, over and over again? How could they expect forgiveness from the man whose life they attempted to take away, countless times? How could they expect their family and friends to be protected, when they have themselves crushed many of the Prophet's *sallallahu 'alayhi wa sallam* kin and companions?

Amid the chaos and the din made of people running and shouting, the Prophet *sallallahu 'alayhi wa sallam* felt the fear around him. He made an announcement: 'Those who shelter in the Ka'bah are safe; those who shelter in the house of Abu Sufyan are safe, and those who remain confined to their houses are also safe.' He then proceeded to the Ka'bah, the *qiblah* (direction) of his prayers. Facing a group of men assembled there, he stopped and asked, 'How do you expect me to treat you?' Quivering, they answered, 'You are a noble man, the son of a noble man!' The Prophet *sallallahu 'alayhi wa sallam* then replied, 'This day no reproach shall be on you. God will forgive you; He is the Most Merciful of the Merciful. Go, you are free. We have not come for war.'

Silence fell over Makkah as relief descended on each and every one of its inhabitants. In a single proclamation, the Prophet *sallallahu* '*alayhi wa sallam*—Mercy to all the worlds—had done what no other conqueror would have done in the circumstance. It was surprising, shocking even, and it was an act of generosity that took everyone off guard. From the crowd, a Qurayshi man came forward and declared: 'O Muhammad, the person I hate the most in the entire of mankind is you.'

Sayyidina Abu Bakr and Sayyidina 'Umar *radhiallahu 'anhuma* were outraged at the statement. In a flash, Sayyidina 'Umar pulled his sword from its scabbard, ready to attack the owner of the ungrateful statement. The companions fumed; after the extreme kindness the Prophet *sallallahu 'alayhi wa sallam* had just shown, was this what the man had to say? 'Put your sword away, 'Umar. We come in peace,' commanded the Prophet. He then turned to the man. 'Why do you hate me?' He asked.

'My heart just hates you, o Muhammad,' the man replied.

The Prophet *sallallahu 'alayhi wa sallam* then asked, 'Can I perform a check on you? Can I touch your chest to see what is in you?' The man shrugged and gave his permission. The Prophet raised his blessed hands, and touched the heart of the man who so arrogantly announced his hatred to the most beloved of Allah subhanahu wa ta'ala.

'O Muhammad!' The man exclaimed seconds later, 'what did you put in my heart? By Allah, I don't love anyone on this earth other than you!'

The Prophet smiled. *Allahumma Salli 'ala Sayyidina wa Habibina wa Syafi'ina Muhammad!*

***

When I first heard the above narration, I couldn't stop crying; how blessed was that man to have his heart checked by the Prophet *sallallahu 'alayhi wa sallam*? How blessed was he that the Prophet's touch was enough to change him from being a cursed person to someone whose iman is complete by his love for the Prophet *sallallahu 'alayhi wa sallam*? As I sat in reflection later that night, Allah *subhanahu wa ta'ala* reminded me of a story I heard weeks before by Ustadha Eiman Sidky:

A non-Muslim western woman crossed paths with a man named Muhammad on her university campus. She fell for his good looks, and did all she could to get close to him. And yet Muhammad—a sincere believer—kept avoiding her, not even looking into her eyes when she stood in his way. Fed up, she confronted him for his perceived arrogance. Muhammad's reply came in the form of a gift of the Qur'an, and later—in answer to her questions on who 'wrote' the Qur'an—a book about the Prophet *sallallahu 'alayhi wa sallam*.

Discovering the character and the mercy of the Prophet *sallallahu 'alayhi wa sallam*, the woman declared that she had fallen out of love with Muhammad, and fallen in love with the one who Muhammad was named after—the Prophet Muhammad *sallallahu 'alayhi wa sallam*. She said the *shahadah*, embraced Islam, and six months later—after countless struggles and tears trying to be the best Muslim she could in a challenging environment—the Prophet Muhammad *sallallahu 'alayhi wa sallam* met her in her dreams.

Allah ...

What struck me was that the woman used to live the stereotypical life of a non-Muslim westerner—clubbing, drinking, being around men all the time—and engaging in one heedless activity after another. And yet, barely six months after she learned about the Prophet *sallallahu 'alayhi wa sallam*, he touched her heart so greatly so that she changed her entire life out of love for him and for Allah subhanahu wa ta'ala (she later married a descendent of the Prophet *sallallahu 'alayhi wa sallam*, as her dream had indicated).

If today it is impossible for us to have our hearts physically touched by the Prophet *sallallahu 'alayhi wa sallam*, like the man of the Quraysh, then perhaps it is as big a blessing to have our hearts touched by his love, character, and stories of mercy ... just like the Muslimah's in the above story.

May Allah subhanahu wa ta'ala place love in our hearts, make us of those who love Him and His Messenger *sallallahu 'alayhi wa sallam*, and make us one of those He loves. Amin.

Afterword

Just so you can have a grasp of the timeline, the above forty letters were written around 2013–2014, when I was approximately twenty-five years of age. Much of their contents were from the time I was pursuing my degree at the International Islamic University of Malaysia in Kuala Lumpur. In contrast, *Ruminations Refined*—my first book—contained reflections from when I was twenty-six to twenty-seven years of age.

Since then, I went on to study full time in a madrasah in Singapore (Rubat Singapura) for a year, before spending close to another year in Tarim, Yemen. The stories from this duration of time in my life? In my next book, *insha' Allah*. Ad du'a bid du'a!

Please feel free to reach out to me through the following channels if you have any feedback, or if you'd just like to read more of my writings:

Instagram: @fadhilahwahid
Facebook: www.facebook.com/nurfadhilah.wahid
Website: www.fadhilahwahid.com
Email: fadhilah.wahid@gmail.com

All errors and mistakes are mine, and all good is from Allah subhanahu wa ta'ala.

Notes and Reflections